COSMIC SPIRIT
THE POWER THAT DRIVES
THE SOFTWARE OF HUMANITY

ALEXANDRA DENNIS

BALBOA.
PRESS

A DIVISION OF HAY HOUSE

Balboa Press books may be ordered through booksellers or by contacting:

Balboa Press
A Division of Hay House
1663 Liberty Drive
Bloomington, IN 47403
www.balboapress.com
1-(877) 407-4847

ISBN: 978-1-4525-3218-9 (sc)
ISBN: 978-1-4525-3219-6 (hc)
ISBN: 978-1-4525-3227-1 (e)

Library of Congress Control Number: 2011900331

Printed in the United States of America

Balboa Press rev. date: 1/28/2011

Many thanks to:
Laura Indovino & Justin Urwin - MBA Office National: Melbourne, Australia
(For assistance in creating the original guidelines for cover jacket design.)

Photography:
© Raquel Pauline Dennis - Melbourne, Australia - 2010. All permissions granted.

Balboa Press Design Team:
David Orr, Katie Schneider, Valerie Deem

For Mum…

And for the loves of my life.

CONTENTS

PREFACE

In writing this book I held strongly onto the concept that I wanted to present helpful spiritual tools that may better enable my fellow human beings to face and navigate their journey through the ongoing challenges that the Life Experience presents before them.

Countless times that I have turned to other Angels on the Earth… for advice, guidance and inspiration. During my lifetime, I have been so blessed with helpful information along the way, that I felt it essential to give something back, release this positive energy out into the Universe.

At various times I have sought counsel from others and although the answers were plain and obvious and their advice most practical, I was often unable to recognize the simplicity of the principles behind the thinking.

Perhaps this was simply because when your "emotional self" is so deeply invested in a situation, it is often difficult to see a matter *clearly and objectively*. Perhaps also at times, I was not ready, too afraid, or did not believe in myself enough. My self esteem was lowered.

I am deeply grateful to all those beautiful flowers of hope that I have met along the way, which have brought me to this point. To all those people along the way who have reminded me of the truth, the authenticity, and the reality that was all too often blurred, hidden behind the veil of fear and anxiety... To all those sweet Souls who are dearest to me, I wish to say a most heartfelt "thank you."

"Thank you, for all the love and light you have showered upon me. For your protection, your guidance and your support..."

And to those more burdened Souls, who have tried to hinder my development, to those who have tried to steal my power, to those who may have felt threatened by my inner beauty and potential, felt the need to hold me down: I say this:

"Thank you, for encouraging the development of my survival instinct, for making me a stronger person. In challenging me, you have helped me to grow. To be strong, to fight with my inner army of courage... and to follow my heart above all."

It doesn't matter how we look on the outside, appearances are simply material based, quite superficial. Although every little thing that we can improve in our external appearance may help improve our level of confidence. So I am all for looking your best, having pride in the appearance, it helps our self-esteem. If you look good, of course you are going to feel better about yourself, so never underestimate the "power" of a new haircut, a relaxing soak in a lavender bath... or a happening new outfit.

If you can look in the mirror and think "Wow!"Look at ME! That looks cool! I'm HOT! I'm fabulous!!!"... Well then you're bound to feel a lot better about yourself.

However, I can give you many examples of many people. Many women, in particular, who may look absolutely gorgeous on the outside, yet are so weak and vulnerable on the inside, that they get pushed and pulled from pillar to post. Blinded to seeing their own "inner beauty", they search approval their whole lives. Once upon a time, one of these women was *me...*

I spent a lifetime of seeking approval, dealing with my abandonment issues, and my violation of trust issues. Living... but NOT really living. Projecting out into the world the notion that I believed I WASN'T GOOD ENOUGH! That I was lacking.
Living in Pain and Fear. Not really living the full life of endless opportunity and potential that I was blessed with when I was born onto this Earth.

Sick and tired of being treated like a doormat, I had finally come to meltdown point. This was not the way I imagined Life to be. I AM worth more, I AM SPECIAL. I count!

Let's affirm: "I recognize, embrace and celebrate the beauty of my own Soul. Not my exterior, but my Soul. I am beautiful, perfect, as Spirit made me, deserving and worthy... EXACTLY as I am."

It does not matter about fitting into SOMEONE ELSE'S pre-conceived IDEAS OF PERFECTION! If you feel bad, you feel bad. But - on the other hand, if you feel good about yourself, and you have a strong sense of DESERVINGNESS and CONFIDENCE, then you can remain "open" to opportunity and greater happiness in your world. Always...MOVE on! *Forward, ahead, into the Future. Forget entertaining negative concepts:*
Simply practice your best smile and move forward!

"There's Life Ahead of Me!"

Not stuck in the Past...
Not hovering there in Limbo–Land...
But FORWARD, with Vision.

I hope this book might help you to assess yesterday, to edit, delete the UNWANTED data, then file it in the file marked "Gone" and farewell your Past...
Put your past in the recycle bin.
See you later... no longer valid!
Time now to envisage a wondrous and although unknown and mysterious, a promising and exciting Future...
To help you make beautiful plans into reality.

And I urge you to GRAB the Now...
Work with all the best tools you can find...
Make it happen!!!
May The Universe bless you, with:
The recognition of *WHO* you truly ARE!

You are Beautiful.
You are Perfection.
You are God.

I don't know if God is a PERSON, or A FORCE, or ALL THAT IS...

Some depict him as a man with a long beard and a white robe, residing on a throne in the clouds...

Some depict him as a jolly laughing rounded-belly guy seeking en-lightenment, as Buddha...

Some imagine him as the Cosmos, The Universe;

Others interpret him as Sky and Sea and Earth and Fire, as the power of the elements, or Nature!

He has many names all over the Globe, and many forms.

You are his eyes and ears on the planet Earth, his legs and arms to move around through your journey, his vision, his ideas, his words, his thoughts, his feelings, his blood in your veins, you are breathing his air.

You are a GOD in Human Form.

The essence of all creation, underneath it all, at its very heart is Spirit.

You are made of the same stuff as are made the Stars.

You are a "being" of Love and Light.

Cosmic Spirit.

You are a being.

Isn't it time you started actually Be-ing!?

Embrace the Now.
And don't worry if you are "different"...

To be different is not to be faulty…
It is to be SPECIAL.
Some of us have always been Different.
Because we are unique individuals.
Find others like yourself and band together in your task.
Greater power in numbers.
Magnify, feel, and amplify the Love.
That's our job on Earth.

ACKNOWLEDGMENTS

I extend the deepest gratitude to The Highest Power of Love and Light... that which some might call God, others may call Source, or Spirit... that of many names and forms, all which translate into Love in the Highest Order. That which made it possible for me to be here incarnate in human form, and whom bestowed the gift of communication through the written/spoken word, the gift of language, of the power of a simple book to enable mass transmission of positive data upon the Earth Plane. I offer this book to all that might seek it, in the Spirit of Goodwill and Happiness.

Thank you... that I am!
I am who I am because God said I am!

To my guiding Ancestors of the realm of yesterday;
To my beloved, supportive family and friends;
To those who belong to the Future in the realm of tomorrow...

Along this journey of through The Eternal Now.
To all the fellow Angels that I have been privileged to know and to have entertained "unawares" along my way.

"Never lose sight of your primary task...
To increase the Light, thus may the shadows diminish and disappear."

Alexandra Dennis.

INTRODUCTION

Welcome…
To the Cosmic Spirit Wireless Light Network!
A Universal Invisible Network…
Of which we are all connected…
A Network constructed purely out of Love and Light,
That which we know as God… that which we all are.
The Light of the Stars.
No wires are required, no GPS, nor phone-lines…
No modems, no routers, no SMS…
Only the KNOWING that we are ALL connected,
Is enough to "register" our spiritual selves and connect with the
Cosmic Spirit…
Through the Mind, Body, Spirit, Soul and Heart.
To log on to the Network.
To harness the Power…
The shared ancient knowledge…
Stored on a giant HARD DRIVE,
The Infinite Resources of an Eternity of Lifetimes…
Of Countless Roles and Identities…
Experiences of Lives lived before…
Of Lives yet to be lived in the after…

And all that IS, that exists forever…
In The Perpetual Now!
The shared memories of FOREVER…
Stored and retrieved via the Giant "Server"…
Otherwise known as God…
The Great Cosmic Spirit

All that exists within it…
Or EMBODIES it in any material Form…
Animal, Vegetable, Mineral…
YOU!
So smile… thinking only loving thoughts…
Embrace your Humanity…
Celebrate your Divinity…

Now "Click Here"…
To Log On!
"Enjoy your Journey."

Welcome!!!

Connecting you now…

To Love and Light Incorporated

Powered by: Cosmic Spirit

The Universal Light Network.

Signal Strength: Excellent.

EMOTION

The Realm of Human Emotion

Water.

Emotions are like water.
Constant, yet ever-changing...
Emotions are the "waters" of our Soul.

Calm, tranquil, smooth sailing.

Rocky, torrential, rough seas.

Glittering turquoise coral reefs… or murky, muddy dams.

Like waves on the ocean, powerful under-currents of "feeling"…
Lapping at the shores of our Souls.
Crashing upon the beaches of our Humanity.

Our own uncharted oceans, our "tides" in synch with the cycles of the
Sun and Moon.

Our lives are made up of many cycles.
Mother Nature's Seasonal Cycles.

The Wheel of Life…
Forever in motion.

Like the Seasons of Nature, our own "Selves" know and have their
own "inner" Seasons.

Our "Winters", seeming endless, can feel so cold, harsh and
unforgiving:

Sadness and sorrow, isolation, depression…

Our "Springs", bringing renewal and re-birth, are new, refreshing,
filled with possibility:

Love and happiness, fertility, potential…

Our "Summers", encouraging enjoyment and fulfillment, they are vibrant and warm:

Elation and celebration, pride, harvest…

And our "Autumns", promoting tranquility and peace, granting us grace and serenity:

Preparation and reflection, hibernation, rest.

Emotions are fluid, like water.

Constant… yet ever-changing.

Think of the many ways we often express feelings, as likened to the seasons or to scales in temperature…

"He was as cold as ice…"
Icy, indifferent, closed, frozen…

"She was burning with desire…"
Hot and steamy, passionate, at boiling point…

Understanding and living with human emotion is like learning to ride the waves of the ocean. Master the waves; otherwise you may drown in a sea of relentless tempest. Make the ocean of emotion your friend.

We must learn to master our emotions, otherwise they may master us. Recognize our emotions for what they are, acknowledge their power as they are occurring, but remember… that they will pass.

Some emotions can feel extremely difficult, like the long "Winter of the Soul"…

But never forget that it can't be Winter *forever!*
It may take a minute, or an hour, or a day, or a week.
It might take/be a year, several years, many years…

Or they can seem like a lifetime.

But it *will* pass.

Ensure you experience ALL the seasons in one day, not just the harshness of our personal Winter.

If you feel stuck in a negative emotion for too long, just mentally take charge, pick a new season, and move on.

Hit delete, and open the mental program…
Open to: "Springtime!"

Remember, like the Melbourne weather…
Our emotions can feel like four seasons in one day…

But it will always change to sunshine again soon!

The Wave

"Let this wave pass
Ride it and feel its power
In the safety of
A mindset that
Reminds me mercifully
That it will pass…
You will be stronger
For its power
You will pass through
A better person
It will challenge you
And defy your strength…
But as the sea
Gracefully retreats
Into a lower tide
You will be calm
And feel the rise
Of your own tidal Spirit…
Let the ripples
Gently smooth
Away your tears
And wash you anew
Clean and vibrant
As the new Sunrise;
It will pass
Of that you can
Be certain."

How emotion differs with the sexes.

Men can master their emotional responses.
They are conditioned to do so as little boys.
In readiness for manhood!

It's no secret that women are very emotional creatures. Men, have a means of controlling emotional responses which is likened to computer security and anti-virus software. Men do not permanently allow themselves to *have* feelings or emotions. While that may sound like a harsh judgment, but in actuality it is apparently a sound and valid statement. Yes, men feel emotions, but they don't allow themselves to INDULGE them for too long, lest they interfere with their ability to be logical, practical, problem-solvers.

What this means is, men have mastered the craft of not actually allowing *constant* emotion to overwhelm them. Emotions are not part of their traditional male make-up. They feel them of course, as they are human-beings, but they don't function with them on a constant and active basis. They feel them sometimes. But they keep them well controlled. This is why women often complain that men are out of touch with their feelings. It's not that they're out of touch; it's just that they have evolved to a level of mental mastery which is required for a man in the competitive world we live in. It's a survival mechanism.
They use this as a method of maintaining clear control of themselves. So that they can be reliable and structured, manly creatures, and they can get things done without the interference or distraction of disturbing emotional currents.

Just like a computer security program quickly detects an unwanted source that may be seeking unauthorized access to the computer system, and blocks it from having access.

Like a security package that is automatically installed in the male psyche, that does not allow entry of harmful data into his system. A male mind works like this when he feels an uncomfortable emotion:

It scans it, analyses it quickly, detects that it might cause the system to malfunction, and therefore shuts down access past a point, to protect the entire system.

Male Emotional Response:
Nip it in the bud!

Males often react directly to the stimulus found within their surroundings. According to the visual or sensual triggers in their environment, they may find an emotion suddenly coming on. They may feel it and then move swiftly to deal with it. They might become upset because they see something sad on TV, like a sick child, and it feels uncomfortable. They might all of a sudden feel the emotion of sadness. They may even find tears welling up in their eyes.

So, they, according to Male Programming, must eliminate that disturbing emotion as quickly as possible.

For example they might then choose to go and do a crossword, or build something out of wood, so that their mind has to focus on thinking of practical matters. Or they might go out into the garden and decide it would be good to cut the lawn, after all, it looks a bit long. That way they can put the sadness out of their head by concentrating on an activity like pushing a lawnmower around. When they are doing the crossword or pushing the lawnmower or attending to a practical task, their mind is freed of disturbing emotional "invaders" again. They know they will be concentrating only on the task at hand and the emotion will disappear from their system.

So, a man's main objective - (when they find an emotion happening) is to eliminate it as quickly as possible by focusing on solving a problem or task of some kind that can occupy their mind fully instead. This is because men generally find emotion to be distasteful, embarrassing, a moment of weakness and distraction from the "really important stuff". A moment of loss of control and of vulnerability. This is why men are often fearful of all- encompassing emotional responses, or love, in general… of things that can really distract them from being in control of their minds.

They are very much displaced through conditioning, from their emotional nature. It is an uncomfortable state and they don't like to feel it. Not for too long. They feel they might lose themselves in the emotional distraction.

It prevents readiness, impedes their ability to have a swift mind, to be on guard, to be essentially, a man!

Women, like men, also react to many triggers in their environment, but even without external stimulus women still have emotions. Triggers are not always required. Emotions for many women are happening continually. Men just allow themselves to have them now and again. They notice them, become aware of them and then deal with getting rid of them. They don't wonder why they are feeling them, they don't want to know. It's their coping mechanism for surviving in a difficult world.

"Why won't this feeling go away?"

Of course at times with males even, there may be really nagging emotions, that keep coming back, or can't be pushed out of their heads. So they then have to go the extra measure of absolutely making sure they don't feel it. If an annoying colleague in the workplace keeps pushing the buttons of a co-worker, a man might try to immerse himself further in his work, so he doesn't have to acknowledge the annoyance. But if it becomes irritating to the point that it can't be ignored the man might have an outburst, say something rude, verbally attacking or in some instances physically expressing their anger.

Sometimes emotion creates a lot of energy within the physical being… that builds up until it requires physical expression. They have need then to vent it, get it out, deal with it, and make it be gone, out, away… from their system.

Escapist Behaviour

The extreme of this of course is an example of why men sometimes go down to the local bar and can go into a binge of drowning their "sorrows" or whatever it is they are finding to be the re-occurring and very disturbing emotion that won't go away. They often turn to escapist behavior like drugs or alcohol - (even sex), to avoid feeling a nagging and persistent emotion that they cannot handle. But it is best to be expressed creatively, ideally. The energy transmuted into a positive expression and released into something PRACTICAL.

Some individuals may seek a method of momentary escape, for a few hours, or days, or whatever the case may be, and as men they can do that.

Because most men are okay in that "de-emotionalized" state. They can absolutely lose all control and escape to "no-where land", and that's okay for them because they are physically strong enough that they can be relatively safe in society - (even in that sedate or relaxed state).

Unless males are very unlucky they aren't going to be attacked or raped while they are in their "out-of-control" de-emotionalized state.

Unlike women. Generally, women cannot afford to use such an escape mechanism without some strong element of risk. Women are not as physically strong, and quite vulnerable in society when in such a state. So women are less likely to place themselves in that predicament unless they have some major and what may seem perhaps to be an insurmountable problem.

Female Emotion
Females live with emotion.
It is what makes for a woman.

Women feel deeply.
They haven't generally mastered the method of controlling their emotional responses.
It is not usually part of women's programming in society.

Some emotions can seem really persistent; feel hugely like enormous "waves" that won't go away. Women generally like to talk about things, or verbally express their troublesome emotions, as that often helps the emotion to lessen in intensity and then be released from the system gently.

For a female to throw her inbuilt sense of caution to the wind and risk being in a vulnerable situation: - (by indulging in escapist activity, or any destructive activity), is not common in an evolved woman. If this occurs then it is a warning sign that she may be finding that the problematic emotion(s) are literally sending her crazy. Round and round and round they go, in her head, never leaving, never going away. Sleepless nights, insomnia, depression, anxiety...

This is why the use of therapy or counseling is so widespread today. People need to verbalize... and then *release* problems, to lessen their internal pressure levels.
"I've got to get this off my chest!"

This is when a person, particularly a woman... needs to phone a friend and discuss it. She needs to hear it outside her own head, verbalize it, acknowledging its power and addressing the issue at hand. The emotional state is telling her something so "loudly" and "clearly" that it cannot be ignored any longer. She has to look at it closer. If this doesn't work, and this method cannot be facilitated, because she's lonely or hasn't got anyone to talk to, perhaps she may risk turning her frustration inward.

Men tend to attack outwardly, venting on their work-mates, arguing with their wife, punching something, having sex, masturbating even; they just have to let the steam OUT!

Women tend to turn their expression INWARDLY; they may undertake self-destructive behavior or put themselves down, start filling their own minds with negative ideas about themselves and become depressed and/or withdrawn.

It is of vital importance that emotions that are troublesome and are building up too much energy within a human body must be dealt with by talking to someone or seeking assistance through counseling. It is not healthy to keep things inside!

This is how disease manifests.

Stress and upset can break down the immune system in the human body and the effect of the problem then has actually become the same as an unwelcome computer virus.

The body has been "invaded" by negative emotional states and thoughts, gradually becoming affected by illness and disease, as it is rendered vulnerable and easily invaded by troublesome energy. This virus-like energy is likened to repetitive and magnified negative thoughts and emotions, which are over-running an otherwise healthy system, weakening it, and causing internally originated physical problems.

The human mind is like a computer.

The mind works like the Central Processing Unit, that gives the commands, houses the memories, orders the files be opened, and works them like a work in progress.

This is Life in human form.

The mind is the platform and our physical form, the linked body… is the rest of the network.

It is the outer housing of the inner CPU.

This body we inhabit is then linked to a greater network, that being the human race.

Mankind: the greatest computer ever created.

Humanity is the network, and it is part of a greater network.

That is called the Universe.

Love and Light Incorporated.

We are all part of it and we welcome you to the knowledge of who you truly are.

A brilliant and fantastic creature.

An intelligent carbon based life-form.

An outlet for God.

He works through us and he is the Big Boss.

Of Love and Light Incorporated.

Our soul, spirit, our life-force…

That which we will call Cosmic Spirit…

Is the power that drives our human mind's software!

In this giant network known as Global Humanity.

We work in conjunction with God…

And perform our tasks.

Store our memories.

We live and breathe and work:

For Love and Light Inc.

It is both our pleasure and our privilege.
In order to be all we can be, we need to understand how things work and take control of our emotions.

They are just re-runs of already stored memories.
Memories which teach us of our learned fears and create our human mind projections of our imagined future happenings.

Pushing through these emotional distractions and embracing only the highest good that our memories serve us to project outwardly, means pushing through our fears, and bravely recognizing our problems as only opportunities and fresh chances, or new beginnings...

For growth and transformational change...

Is vital.

Moving forward in the positive is our mission statement:

At "Love & Light Inc."

Our objective is to solve and eliminate problems quickly so as to greater be able to perform of Earthly tasks as they were meant to be, in the most positive means.

We aim for...
THE HIGHEST GOOD OF ALL CONCERNED.

And God is our Compass!

SOS:

OR... When problems aren't detected early and dealt with...

"Help Me!"
A person who cannot cope with an emotion she keeps having and cannot have the message or problem acknowledged or addressed will feel very alone. She may over-eat, gamble, smoke a cigarette, and cut her hair. All this behavior is defined as acting out in destructive mode. So negative. How can we stop this from happening?

In the old movies someone would slap the person and shout "Pull yourself together!"

If it can't be done, hypnosis is a useful tool in deleting troublesome files from the mind and reprogramming with positive, helpful, wise data.

People can read books, they can stick signs up all around their house, they can take the gentle approach, spend years in therapy, but it's simply self-indulgent negativity and at some stage the individual may become so tired of feeling bad that they simply ELECT to move forward.

SELF ESTEEM is a huge factor as well as past programming, negative childhood memories, all of that...

But at some stage one has to say to themselves:
I want a positive change.

Thus they are welcomed back on board at Love & Light Inc. and they resolve to strive and move forward as part of a team.

Here's an example of a person being lost in the tornado of unresolved emotions and negative self-talk due to perhaps negative programming in the past:

Can you see that the only one being affected and hurting is the person indulging in the negative fantasy?

A person might convince herself that they are too fat, or old or ugly or unintelligent, literally run themselves down verbally while talking to themselves in the mirror.

They may do this because they are compounding the idea that they ARE all these things, because if they weren't, then they'd surely have a companion around who cared enough to listen. They might have been told negative things about themselves in childhood. They might have believed all those things they heard. They need to understand that the person who said them was only projecting their OWN inadequacy and as a result was perhaps unaware of the damage they were inflicting through negative words going into an impressionable mind. A mind who can't process and establish those words a truth yet because they lack the maturity or life-experience, and therefore embrace whatever they are told and store it in their memory bank as being the uncontested truth and gospel. The negative programming has leaked into yet another system and is doing untold damage.

It needs to be stopped.
Look into the mirror and reprogramme.
Wipe the old files out that are continuing to spread the virus.

Delete and salvage and start afresh
New programming,

Caution:
IF THIS VIRUS IS NOT DETECTED & REMOVED: SYSTEM
CRASH!

These negative emotions, if they are troubling enough, MUST be released from one's system.

One might begin to feel as though their head might explode otherwise.

It is vital to find POSITIVE WAYS to express energy or emotion.

AND THIS IS WHY:

EMOTION × PRESSURE:

"Sitting" on an issue for a long time without resolution…

Or a continuing emotion experienced over and over and over – without any release)…

A MAGNIFICATION OF THE EMOTION OVER TIME…
Equals ENERGY.

Energy that is real, powerful, and can be put to use.
POWER!

That is why it is VITAL that only positive energy use is facilitated.

It is the number one rule at Love & Light Inc.

We would like to imagine that energy created from our inner state of being, thought and emotion…

That this POWER can be harnessed and put to proper use.

Ideally… for POSITIVE and CREATIVE purposes.

Powerful Energy like that is potent… and should be well respected.

There is a formula below that illustrates such a dynamic:

EMOTION × INFINITY/INTENSITY/PRESSURE = ?

Think about it for a moment.

A FORMULA FOR POWER 2

How Energy Moves ... Is Directed & Exchanged

EMOTION × TIME = ENERGY/POWER

The formula for Power!

Put simply, the symbolism included in the equation is represented as such...

1) *"Emotion" symbolized by the teardrop – (ie: Water of our Soul)...*

2) *Magnified or multiplied by...*

   (strengthened by continuous concentration, & infinitely subjected to pressure... thus the Infinity symbol -the "Lemniscate")...

   aka: the passage of "TIME"....

3) *Equaling "Energy" –*
   (symbolized here by the Japanese POWER symbol.)

POTENT POWER:

Sexual Energy
Sexual Energy is the most potent form of energy exchange that exists on the Earth Plane.

After all, the act itself can CREATE LIFE!

Sex – As an act of "Release"
A lot of men have sex for this purpose. Look at the bodies of males and females. Men have a penis, it's an emptying device. It is designed to vent, to empty, to discard, to evict or eject, if you like, "energy" from the system, OUT into the world. It is an energy dispatcher, a releaser.

Therefore, males are very strong TRANSMITTERS OF ENERGY.

If males are able to relax and *allow* themselves to receive, they can also be RECEIVERS.

Sex – As an act of "Receipt"

Now look at the female, she has a vagina, it's a receptacle. It's surely a receiver, and all the energy she captures, absorbs and stores and distributes within herself.
INTERNALISING, TAKING IN!

Therefore, women are very strong RECEIVERS OF ENERGY.

Women too, feel like they might explode, but where's the "energy" going to go??? It's like a pressure cooker. It can be released, but not through her vagina into the world like a man does. It can be concentrated and released, but it MUST be released POSITIVELY!

Therefore women can also be TRANSMITTERS.

How men can help women.

That's why men should encourage women to talk, because they get their negative "data input out" by talking and releasing. That is the useful venting mechanism. Women, in fact, most people, regardless of sex, don't need to be "fixed".

They just need to be heard.

Many worried men want to run a mile when a woman has a problem, because first of all they assume it's their fault. Plus they don't feel very enthused about having to deal with someone else's uncomfortable or often *"messy"* emotions.

It might feel disgusting, very uncomfortable, or unnatural. So the more they try to run away from the female, the more her energy inside will turn negative and in fact can magnify and rebound anyway onto the man.

So it's very important for men to listen and for people to verbalize, work through and communicate issues, so that they can be brought into the light of day and thus healing and release can begin to take place.

To listen impartially, without judgment, without taking personal offense, is an art-form, one that allows for the highest healing to take place.

If it is difficult to listen to another's problems but you would like to assist, visualize WHITE LIGHT encompassing you in your mind's eye. See it as a huge cocoon of protective white light, like a force-field surrounding you.

This will enable you to listen and help, without too much negative residue rubbing off on your own aura.
REMEMBER:
UNRESOLVED ISSUES CONTINUE TO BUILD ENERGY!

There is no such thing as sweeping "matters" under the carpet!

Eventually the carpet develops a hill underneath it and eventually someone is going to stumble upon that hill and fall down!

Energy in motion:

A powerful release of emotionally charged energy, aimed towards an object or result.

Remember:

$$\text{EMOTION} \times \text{TIME} = \text{ENERGY}$$

Warning! Women and Energy…
Without even realizing it, your teeny, gentle, unassuming sweet woman could possess such an intensity of energy build-up within her system, bursting to come out!
It can, if encouraged to be generated for positive effect.

Equally simply, if it's rejected and unacknowledged by her significant male counterpart - (ie: husband/partner), it may fester away silently and without any visible clues…

Into a cyclone of negativity and be directed without control towards the person she deems should receive it.
This is why when men ignore women's feelings they can get so angry.
Over-reacting.
Overwhelmed.
Because the issue that might be originally 9 on a 1-10 problem scale…
then magnifies directly in proportion to her rejection…
into 999,999,999 in about 3 seconds flat!

Isn't it better to listen patiently, with concern wisely...?
BEFORE the volcano erupts!?

When a woman says she needs to talk, the quicker she's heard then instantly the smaller the problem becomes. When a woman can, they will try to work through an issue herself. But sometimes she may need help with it.

This built up energy has to go somewhere...
It needs to be EXPRESSED.
Better that it is released gently, through healthy exchange.

In general, females can effectively deal with and live with MOST of their emotions – (of moderate kinds).

Because for a woman...

Emotions are a huge *part of her life*, her entire being.

Having said before that males don't PERMIT emotions all the time – (they just experience them now and again)...

I will emphasize now that women have them...
 Non-stop.

Women live with EMOTIONS CONSTANTLY HAPPENING AND ACTIVE...

So yes, for women, life is like living with an internal constantly active volcano!

Generally, Men have five senses. Women have six. Like men, women have Sight, Taste, Smell, Sound and Touch. But women, particularly, have a sixth sense.

That sixth sense is represented by their emotional self. It is the realm of feelings, insight, intuition, guidance & teachings, telepathy and other psychic abilities. It is the mysterious, unproven, immeasurable, not-explained-easily-by-science "sense".

Some males are more aware of the presence of their "extra sense", but are somewhat uncomfortable with this aspect of their nature. Males are far more practical in their thinking and don't like their emotional side to over-ride their rational thinking processes.

"Little boys DON'T cry!"
The main reason why males are less in touch with their feeling side is this. As little boys males are programmed to ignore their emotions. They are told "Little boys DON'T cry!"

This is because they are expected to grow up one day as a strong man, capable of protecting his mate. Adult males are expected to be the "backbone" of a family unit. The father, husband, pillar of strength. How secure could a wife and children feel if the head of the household kept bursting into hysterical tears every five minutes when something went wrong?

Men are forced to ignore their gentle and sensitive side and get with the program of being a big, strong, macho dude! They don't talk about their problems to other males, even their own friends.

Because, just like in the animal kingdom, other males – (even their best buddies) are seen as "opponents" or competitors in the game of human survival.

Men are primal creatures; their systems acknowledge and react according to the most basic drives.
The Basics!

Hunger, sleep, sex!
Hungry... Must eat!
Tired... Must sleep!
Horny... Must have sex!

That's basically it.
It's not an insult, it's just how they are made!
They don't need much else to survive.
It's their hardwired instinctual MALE programming.

Males may think that if they tell even their closest "buddy" a problem of theirs... that they are rendering themselves weak, vulnerable and open to attack.

Men think like animals in the wild.

Those men who do not conform to such a simplistic attitude or outlook on life, who may perhaps have strong creative or artistic inclinations, poets, writers, artists, musicians, and the like... are often accused of being UNMANLY. It is because these activities are usually emotionally driven and they are more in touch with their feminine side, creative side, and emotional undercurrents striving for expression.

These gentler spirited males are also in touch with their sixth sense, (as most women already are).

The greatest beauty can be created when men are not afraid to allow their inbuilt "guarding mechanism" or their emotional wall down, and to bravely allow their feelings to emerge.

Emotion then transmutes into energy, and their inspired work is brought to life with true FEELING.

To transmit feeling and inspirational thought into actual creation...

Through and into physical form.
From inside to outside.
From the inner to the outer.

Incredible beauty.

Survival of the Fittest!
In the Animal Kingdom, if a stray Lion thinks the big old Lion is looking a bit worse for wear, he might have a go at him and take over the pride.

He might challenge him in a moment of weakness and claim the lionesses as his own. He usually will then proceed to eat the cubs — (because *they aren't his own*), in an attempt to preserve his superior gene-pool.
He will mate with the lioness to produce his own genetically SUPERIOR cubs!

Men think like that.

So, they keep their problems in their own head, like to sort their "stuff" out for themselves, and most of all…

There's a tight lid clamped down on their emotions.
They have made an art-form out of SUPPRESSION!

Emotions are weakness, they make for distraction.
They can make a man … (after all, a mere mortal) –
Lose complete control of himself.
A man fears, in the deepest parts of his mind, that he might lose everything that defines who he is and what is his… If he doesn't keep those nagging emotions well in check.

Men learn this self-protection mechanism from early on in childhood. Self Preservation. This strong male survival instinct is inbuilt because the continuation of a male's heritage or "bloodline"… depends upon it!

Perhaps that is why:
A man in allowing for the floodgates to give way to strong emotion, and sixth sense, and further to express it creatively… is sadly often perceived by greater society as being homosexual.

Perhaps then, to truly allow ones-self to feel… (as a man) – is likened to renouncing one's manhood?!

LOVE

The Highest Power

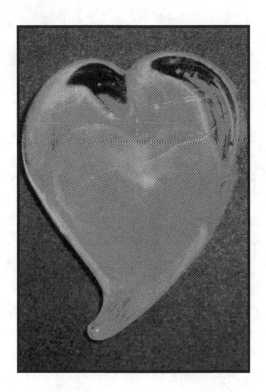

Love is all there is.

Love is "Energy".

Love is the "Highest Vibration" in the known Universe.

The Colour associated with Love in its purest form is Pink. Strongly associated with Love is Rose Quartz, which is to be found in nature and comes only in various shades of Pink.

Different Types of Love

There are two different types of love:
1) Type 1 is CONSTANT.
2) Type 2 is DYNAMIC: (ie: "energy pushing", but NOT constant).

Type 1 – CONSTANT / (Love for Someone):
"I love you…"

Type 1 is Love that is well established from early on. It is the type of unconditional Love that you would have for your parents, children, relatives, best friends, or your long-term partner. It is strongly founded and doesn't alter; it is always there, constant.

Type 2 – DYNAMIC / (Romantic Love):
"I'm *IN love* with you…"

Type 2 is Love that has not been so well founded, is usually in its early stages, and relates to the love felt between two sexual (ie: potential mating) partners. This type of Love is not usually felt for friends or relatives and is charged with chemical attraction. This type of Love is accompanied with intense physical feeling and is part of the human mating process. It often changes after a period of time. It either fizzles out or dies into nothingness, (ie: they break up) – or it relaxes gradually into a more secure, less intense, but probably more solid type of Love.

Actually, to be specific, it changes into Type 1 Love.

If you equate these types of Love to waves on the ocean, or to water:

Constant Love (Type 1) is like a gentle paddle down a steady, flowing, serene stream…

Dynamic Love (Type 2) is like a torrential storm, with huge tidal waves…
Or canoeing on a river with a wild and unpredictable torrent, hidden waterfalls and rocky yet thrilling rapids.

Love is the greatest Power on Earth.
Love is a powerful Healer.
The power of Love can overcome most obstacles. Love is stronger than the ills of the world, it is greater than Fear.

Authentic Love
Type 1 Love, or Constant and Unconditional love is what a parent feels for *a child*.

A parent's Love for their child is probably the *TRUEST, PUREST, REALEST* form of Love on the planet.

As Human Beings, we may never experience a more authentic version of Love.

This type of Love can move mountains, overcome darkness, offer protection and safety; it can create and eternally maintain a sound and peaceful mindset.

A feeling of security... of "belonging".
It offers a "Home".
The Home of the Heart.

Take My Heart

The gift of a heart that's given freely is the most precious gift that a human being can offer another human being on the Earth Plane. When Love is offered unconditionally, the "Giver" is symbolically offering the "Receiver" their Heart.

This "gift" is offered with the understanding of an unspoken yet valid expectation of spiritual loyalty.

This "Agreement of the Heart" includes the mental clause that it will be retained in "safe keeping" and spared from mistrust, deception and hurt.

When these rules are violated and broken, the original "owner" of the Heart will feel the impact of the damage as spiritually and absolutely realistic, just as if their Heart had been torn out, broken, stolen, smashed on the ground, or turned to stone.

This "pain" we know to be the syndrome of...
"The Broken Heart".

It is real, destructive, damaging and devastating. Over time, if it cannot be healed, it can result in the manifestation of illness in the physical form.

We must be very selective and careful about those whom we choose to entrust our Heart to in this Lifetime, for a violation of this trust can be powerful enough to destroy the human Spirit.

A Broken Heart
When a heart is broken, a little piece of the Heart is retained by the "breaker".

Compounded over time, this "missing piece" can develop from a tiny dent or pinprick hole into an eternal void of emptiness harboured within the Soul. If this cannot be addressed, healed, or repaired in some way, it can eat at the human Spirit like a cancer.

Damage Control
There are many resources out there in the world that we can utilise: therapists, doctors, religious movements, and the like. But if you find that nothing is helping, you need to go to the "breaker" and confront them.

If you are able, if they are *still in mortal form upon this planet*, you *MUST* face them bravely and make them acknowledge the impact of their actions, demand that they be accountable for the "damage".

It does not mean you have to lash out in anger, because that type of behaviour is only compounding a negative act, and heals nothing. You must, however, talk to the "breaker" about what has occurred, and make them *see* that it has had a lasting result. You must *ASK* for your Heart back. Fully intact.

Spiritually you owe it to yourself to "take" back the broken fragments and "*replace*" them as best you can. Be assertive in asking for the co-operation of the "breaker" in this process.

Note: Because the "breaker" may feel threatened by your decision to confront them, they may *refuse* to co-operate. However, simply by the act of confronting them, you have already begun to re-claim your "power", and you will *accelerate* the healing process.

Dammit! You count!

DESERVINGNESS!

"Deservingness", or our mental level of deservingness…
Worthiness, self-esteem, confidence.

These are the greatest factors in our ability to achieve our Heart's deepest desires.

SMASH THROUGH OLD PATTERNS!

If we can find the balance between assertiveness and aggression, or confidence and pushiness… If we can remember that we COUNT, we *deserve* to be happy in Love, then we create the perfect environment for a MIRACLE to take place.

Sometimes…
Even against the most challenging odds, a MIRACLE can happen in our Lifetime.

LOVE CAN MOVE MOUNTAINS!
Believe it.

The Message

"Lady Love
Came unto him
And whispered
To his ear

Heed well
My cryptic song
For it shall soon
Become quite clear

Fear not young man
Give all yourself
Succumb
To natures call...

For only
Once you've loved
Can you conceive
That love is All."

FEAR

The Mental Road Block

The opposite of Love... is Fear.

Fear is a "Mechanism".

It's a "block" – a self-created block... preventing us from stepping forward into greater Light.

Fear has no power of its own. Fear is only "fuelled" by our own feelings of self-doubt.

Fear is natures inbuilt safety equipment. It is a "caution" sign. But if we can't recognise this fact, it can seem like a rigid, absolute "Do Not Enter" sign. If we can't see the flexibility in this mechanism of caution, it can control us.

Some years ago, after many disastrous relationships and what seemed and felt like a lifetime's worth of collateral damage, disappointment and pain...
I found myself beginning to fall head over heels in Love.
It caught me by surprise.
When I wasn't looking.
Snuck up on me.

I never thought it possible, but it was a powerful chemistry and I could feel myself slowly succumbing to its power.

As soon as the potential for hurt raised its ugly head within me, as soon as I realised that my feelings were out of control, as soon as I realised this could be "the One"... I set out to push the person away, out of my Life.

To destroy the potential "threat".

This familiar dynamic relates to my well-learned mental cycle:
An old pattern of thought which I used to entertain...

"Intimacy equals vulnerability... equals violation of trust... equals pain." So, watch out.

I used to try to visualise or imagine myself being happy in an embrace with this beautiful man, but every time I did this, half way through… his face would turn into a gruesome monsters face, or he'd attack me, anyway… it would end up being a scary and traumatic scenario.

No matter how hard I tried to OVER-RIDE this mechanism, I could not beat it! It was obviously bigger than my desire for intimacy.

Otherwise I would act in a way that would deceive the person into thinking that I wasn't really that interested in him. I was SO afraid of allowing him to KNOW how much I really loved him.

In the end, I drove this person away. Then I spent the next few years crying about it and wishing he'd please come back.

If only I could have ONE more chance…
At Love.

Yet I, myself, had created it. Due to my own Fear.

When fear like this comes into play, we need to sit and think hard about the grounds for such fear. If it really seems like a danger sign to you, rather than a more flexible caution sign, then you need to ask yourself what the fear is about. What is it telling you? That your circumstances are inappropriate, that you ought to turn and take another direction, that the path ahead of you is "inappropriate", or that simply you are not spiritually healed or "ready" enough to take a step forward in this direction?

T- Intersections & Road Blocks
Imagine Life as walking a straight line, when a "caution sign" appears ahead of you, you are supposed to think about it. Do I veer off the

path, turn left or right? Because it's a cross-roads. It may seem like a T-intersection, but is it REALLY? Or is it a self-imposed Road Block?

It was *definitely* a road block in my case, clearly that I perceived to be there, because I was terrified of proceeding on the path that I sensed lay ahead. Perhaps it was too soon for me. Merely months earlier I'd only *just* experienced and survived the major melt-down of a recent divorce. *Watch out… too soon…*

Do Not Enter… Wrong Way, Go Back!
Perhaps the intersection ahead of me was simply, just that. A CROSSROADS?

But, in Fear, I preferred to SEE it as a ROAD BLOCK.

NO ENTRY!
In the middle of the night, while my Fear was rampant, I dispatched a mental "crew" of road workers in their reflective wear, who went and set up my Road Block, so that when I woke up in the morning, there was suddenly a "DO NOT ENTER" sign there and the road was *BLOCKED OFF!*

Some people may feel "brave" enough to jump in and have a go at it, but even then, they seem to find ways to ensure the relationship doesn't "progress" as it potentially could. They are sick of being alone, crave company, feel ready enough to have a little shot at a relation-ship, but STILL need a lot of healing before they can take down the remaining "road blocks".

Unco-operative Behaviour
Here's a classic scenario:

"My partner is so irresponsible, he spends all his money, never has any regard for bills or any important things, he never spends any time with me, and he avoids intimacy…"

This behaviour is based upon Fear, especially if a person has had a succession of broken relationships, marriage break-down and previous children…

People who are actively involved in relationships yet keep displaying behaviours that are irresponsible or hindering to the progress of the relationship as a "productive unit", are using their un-co-operative behaviours and hindering activities as a "road block".

A self-imposed road block to ensure that they can't succeed…
In simply BEING HAPPY.

Because of existing "baggage" from previous unsuccessful relationships, they find never-ending "excuses" to impede their present relationship's further development.

Overcoming strong Fear like this is extremely difficult.
Sometimes IMPOSSIBLE.
Often the only remedy for this type of Fear, is Time.
Time…a powerful Healing Force.
Only surpassed in its power, by Love.

At times I wonder whether I will ever truly know the difference between a true intuition of danger (in Love or otherwise), or an ongoing Fear. Fear of being fulfilled in Love?

Self Sabotage

Self sabotage is a mechanism that comes into the picture to prevent one's self from succeeding in something that they really want to achieve but feel they *do not* DESERVE.

Self sabotage is our way of messing things up because our low level of self-esteem or deservingness makes us believe that we are not worthy of accepting good things or being happy. It's self punishing behaviour.

Fear of Success Vs. Intuition?

One might ask themselves, were all those missed opportunities or failed attempts at relationships actually NOT right for me anyhow? Were they simply not "meant to be"?
Or am I seriously damaged and afraid?

The greater the level of damage and/or baggage a person holds in their life, the more that Fear comes into play.
That's why, if we can mentally "clean house" and travel light, so to speak, we give ourselves a better chance of success.

Commitment Phobia is a situation caused by giving up one's power to Fear. Fear... that you don't have what it takes, to make it "work". Fear that you're "not up to it..."

This is when Fear challenges Love, and wins out!
Or we, as human beings, ALLOW it to.

Often, we break our OWN Hearts... before anyone *else* can.

Yesterday

"Yesterday I held it within my hands
Never knowing that his treasured heart
All the while it was there simply for the enchanting
Somehow, it slipped away while I hesitated
So strange it felt to know this tenderness
Frightened by the power of an emotional sea
Unfathomable depths so dangerous yet magnificent
If only I could let myself jump in and swim
To brave the waves and journey them home
For me the fear was strong that surely there must be
A hidden catch for there had to be something
Wrong... for it to feel so right
The product of a history that taught me so severely
To believe that I did not deserve to be happy
That taught me so painfully to be suspicious of
Whatever made me feel something warm
The seedling so well ingrained in my being
Of self-sabotage so deeply rooted had grown
Into a tree that was actually a weed disguised
Within myself that could not be pulled
It has cost me dearly those things I've most loved
Afraid to replenish the barren garden of my spirit
To let the rainfall gently cleanse my soul
Afraid to expose my heart to a stranger
The most treasured gifts I implored of the Universe
I rejected as fiercely as I had once prayed for them
To push away the potential pain
Of love that hit me like a tidal wave

In surprise and horror all at once
It is I who perplexed have duly learned
Now since he has been lost to another
Who swims in his sea bathing in the moonlight
Of his eyes each night
While I afar wonder if he knows
I love him more now because he is vanished
For there is sweet safety and beauty to be found
Within the sanctuary of loving in distance."

Overcoming Fear

Fear has no power of its own. The way you react to Fear gives it "Energy". As the famous saying goes:

"There is nothing to Fear, but Fear itself!"

When you can eliminate Fear, there is Love.
Fear is Black.
Negative…
Has no Colour.
No Light.
Fear is the absence of Love and Light.
Mentally learn to recognise Fear as it is happening, and "ask it to leave".

Affirm:

"I am Fearless!"

"I am… strong, confident, beautiful, intelligent, intuitive, happy, healthy and sound of mind."

"I am blessed with good fortune, prosperity and the gifts of Love and Light".

Forsaking all else and otherwise.

Fear will follow you, if you let it, like a shadow. Unless you turn your back on it. Delete "Fear"… It doesn't serve you.

"Keep facing the Light and you will never see the shadows..."

Fear would like to bring you undone. So rise above it. Build a bridge and get over it. Move forward, leave Fear behind. It's like the "weak link".
The crippler!

Guilt, shame, regret...
Fear.

These things are not designed to enhance our potential; they are designed to control us, to keep us down, dark and broken.

Break the chains of Fear.

As long as we are not hurting anyone, we should feel free to live our lives the best way we know how to.
Mindful of... RESPONSIBILITY.

"I've gotta' do, what I've gotta' do."

Be true to yourself. Only you, no-one else. As long as we can be mindful and respectful of the Law of Karma, we can live our own lives. Move forward, with responsible choice in mind.

With Free Will. Responsible Choice.

You are free to choose your own version of Happiness!

Freedom

"The wonderful sound
Of being alone
No angry voices
No demanding phone
Strangers in love
All around me
Embracing in silence
So touching to see
I drink to my freedom
It tastes just divine
The spirit of liberty
Mixed with my wine
Tonight will allow
For me to be me
Without restricting
My potential to be."

The "Right" Choice

It may not be "right" for others – (ie: friends, family etc), but if it is "right for us", then we deserve to do so. Otherwise, your imagined "sense" of responsibility and obligation may brew over time into a built up cess-pool of resentment and bitterness.

Resentment privately harboured towards those whom you "imagined responsibility".

When the Love of my Life moved to a new home in Queensland, thousands of miles away from my home city of Melbourne, I felt as though he had deserted me.

His personal reasons for moving were irrelevant, I felt rejected, un-loved and unworthy. Immediately, my desertion and abandonment issues – (ie: "Fear") jumped into play. So I found reasons to magnify my negative attitudes.

Negativity and Fear breeds Negativity and Fear.
"I'm not good enough!"

I mentally decided that I could *not* join him in his new location, due to the "imagined sense of responsibility" to my family. After all, I had a Mother who had been seriously ill, and I felt that I ought to live nearby to her, in case she needed my help.
Over the next few years, I visited him several times, but I always left without any sense of resolution. He must have tired of my "games"… But my Fear was SO powerful.

Fear of Love!

Years passed by, and I still I felt trapped in Limbo-Land.

Then one day…
I heard that he had "moved on", I felt my Heart SNAP in two! I completely lost the plot.

He was GONE…
"Owwwccchh!"
Clearly, he had moved on, with Time…
But MY Heart had *not* moved on.

My physical body had stayed put in Melbourne.
And my spirit was lost somewhere in between…

A Lost Soul.

The irony of this tale is that years later, my Mother visited the *"other"* city several times for vacation, fell in love with it, and thought it was absolutely wonderful. She contemplated moving there HERSELF.
I felt like a LOSER…
For letting the opportunity slip through my fingers.
Due to "imagined obstacles"…

You can just imagine *how ridiculous* I felt?
And how *annoyed with myself* I was!

But the Love of my Life…who by this point had gently evolved into an old friend, rather than a "missed opportunity", lovingly counselled me through it.
We concluded together… that "TIMING" is everything…

And if things are meant, then they will be.

Still, I took an incredible life lesson from this course of events.
I KNEW then, that I would never allow that to happen again.
I couldn't blame anyone but myself.
You learn much from loss.
You learn to hang on to the things you really Love.
You learn to live in the NOW, and embrace and savour your blessings.

TO PUSH THROUGH FEAR.
TO BRAVELY STEP FORWARD.

Fear is designed to caution us, within reason.
But if we allow Fear to control our lives we may find ourselves "Stuck in Limbo". Afraid to take decisive action.

Time may feel like it can stand still for us.
But while we are trapped in the "prison" of Fear... Time moves forward.
Chronologically, on this Earth Plane we inhabit.

We age.
Life goes on.
And we can easily become "stuck".
Only *WE* hold the "Magic Key".

No-one's going to rescue us if we don't help them to find the Key. If we aren't prepared to hand it over, how can they release us from our bonds of Fear? Sometimes the "Key" symbolically resides on a chain around our own necks. If we could only see that it might be hanging there, over our Heart Chakra.

A Key.

Think about it... like a Cross.
Many wear one around their necks.
A crucifix!
It can represent our BURDEN.

Or, ideally... it can represent our FAITH.

FAITH...

The Magic Key
Like the "cross", which often is used a symbol of our Faith.

Yet, sadly, too often, this which should represent our Faith,
Is often connected with feelings of Fear.
Guilt, shame...
Conventional and organized religion...
Don't do this or that... as GOD will get you!
You will be punished!

Boundaries.
Rules.
Imposed upon us.
To control us.

HOW IS THAT REALLY ABOUT GOD AT ALL?
SCARING PEOPLE INTO SUBMISSION TO A SET OF
RULES...
HOW CAN THAT BE POSITIVE AT ALL?
How can that encourage qualities such as:
Confidence, spiritual growth, good self-esteem...

Or any reasonable trust in one's own judgement and choice?

It just breeds doubt, fear and limitation of scope.
Even if God doesn't punish us, some people might think that we should punish ourselves.
That we don't DESERVE to be happy.
Because we might have been "BAD" in the eyes of the local priest once...
When we confessed that we told a fib...
Or fought with a sibling...
Or threw a tantrum as a child.
Or something similar, which in realistic retrospect...
Is petty, tiny and irrelevant.

NEGATIVE PROGRAMMING SO OFTEN STICKS...
When compounded from so many directions and sources into a young mind...
It can ruin lives!

Let's be gentle with ourselves and eliminate the negative self-talk.

DELETE WHAT DOESN'T SERVE YOU...
LET IT BE GONE FROM YOUR LIFE.

We must trust in ourselves that we are good people, of high ideals.

We must believe in ourselves.
Trust in our ability to be wise and fair.
To be reasonably discriminating and discerning, yet open-minded and humanitarian in our outlook towards Life.
Towards humanity.

If we wish to harm none…

If we wish only to act out of Love and Light,
If we wish to grow,
If we wish to be all that we can be…

Then… YES! We can overcome our Fears and be *truly* great.

Other Peoples Fear

Sometimes other people can hold us back from being all we could potentially be. We must not allow them to limit our true potential. We must move forward. They can come on the journey with us; they are welcome to join us.

But if it is too daunting a path for them, we should still go. But only… if we realise we may be going on that journey alone, and we feel brave enough to make the journey alone.

If the destination is your "dream", you may make detours along the way. You may be distracted and busy, but never lose sight of your "dream".

Our Destination?

This is where the word *"Destiny"* is derived from. Destiny… Our true path.

If we can find a gentle sense of equilibrium that will keep us centred and mindful of our destination, we can ease along *towards* it.
But remember, NEVER to *force* it.

If you force something that isn't fitting naturally, it will break.

Move with Mother Nature.
Go with the Flow...
Don't rush.
Don't dawdle.
Just put one foot in front of the other.

Step through Fear.

It has no power.

TIME

The Key to the Universe

Timing is everything.

Some say Past, Present and Future are all insignificant...
That ALL are occurring simultaneously.

Just imagine that someone steps out of the clouds and hands you a sparkling, golden Key.

They instruct you to guard it well, to hold onto it and wait... because in time it will open a mysterious door that is the door that leads to your *Destiny*.

Time is that Key.

Imagine further, that you try to use your special Key to open a door, but it's locked.
You go back to that door, over and over, because you just KNOW that what's behind it is something really fantastic! You are a bit scared to open it because you don't know if there'll be a booby-trap waiting to get you behind that door, but you are feeling brave enough to take that chance.

You go back to the door, because you are CONVINCED that behind it is what you need to see. It's all the treasures you've ever imagined, in a great big chest, glimmering gold and jewels, just waiting there for you to discover.

But the door won't unlock, because it's been encoded with a safety mechanism, an alarm, and a timing device. Like a safe.
Set on a timer.... Unable to be cracked.
A tough nut to crack!

So...All you can do is wait.
When the Time is right, if you still hold the Key, the prize will be yours.
Time.

Like the lock on our "secret locked door" and our hidden treasure-chest…
Don't force it. It will open when the Time is right.

The Apple Tree

Things happen at their own Time. To everything there is a cycle, and Nature is a fine example of this.

Just because you want to eat an apple right at this moment, doesn't mean that you can demand it of the apple tree. Don't go yelling and screaming at the apple tree "I want an apple… NOW!"

It makes no difference.

The apple tree will produce an apple when it feels like it's ready to.

Not just because *YOU* want one *right now*.

Things happen when they are meant to.
What will be, will be.
In Time.

No-one need worry about fitting into some pre-contrived schedule regarding their own life.

If all your friends are settling down, they have spouses and children...

Yet you cannot find the "One" and still there are no children about...

DON'T take it on board that you're a failure...

DON'T convince yourself there must be something wrong with you.

DON'T fall into the trap of feeling DIFFERENT, ABNORMAL, FLAWED!

This is negative self-talk.

It can happen when we observe others around us and make the mistake of COMPARING our OWN lives to theirs.

NEVER do this to yourself.

We ALL have our OWN time-frames for the MILESTONES in
our lives.
We don't live on ANYONE ELSE's Schedule...
Tell yourself...
Remind yourself:
"This is MY Life... and No-one else's!"
This is MY OWN personal journey.
THE MIND:

It all starts in the Mind.
Whatever we have created in our environment
All stems from the Mind

Our Mind is the Guardian of our Heart.
Our Mind can trick us when it wants to protect us.

It says: "Don't go that direction!"

Or: "Yeah, I've assessed a situation and I conclude THIS about it!"

So... THIS is my TRUTH!

This is my spin on it.
This is what I gather/feel/see... from MY perspective.
This is my surveillance of the scene... and my drawn conclusion on
the matter.
This is what I SEE, based on my personal SCOPE.
This is what my VISION registers as true and valid, based on my
observations.

Often there is a BIGGER picture, than simply what we can see ourselves.

We only get a little zoomed in scope of the whole picture.

Some of us like to try to zoom out and see more.

Some of us might try to ZOOM OUT... with our MIND'S EYE!

Some of us might see more than is IMMEDIATELY VISIBLE.

With our IMAGINATION.

When zooming out...

Keep the feelings positive.

IMAGINE...

With the highest good as your intention.

IMAGINATION IS OUR HUMAN GIFT...

IF WE CAN SEE IT, IT IS BECOMING REAL.

WE ARE CRAFTING IT ALREADY INTO MATERIAL FORM.

The Blueprints are being drawn as we imagine.

When someone draws a blueprint for the construction of a physical structure, like a building – for example:

They aren't going to design one that looks terrible and is bound to collapse.

That would be ridiculous!

So when you draw up your mental blueprints...

Make them solid and spectacular.

Make them sturdy.

Ensure they promote good feelings and positive use.

Remember:

If you imagine monsters...
They EXIST for you.

But... If you imagine HEAVEN on Earth...
With all possibilities before you and with an open heart...

YOU WILL CREATE IT BEFORE YOU.

Before you, which means in the Future.

Use your Heart...
When stepping into your Future.

Let it be your compass and your map...
Your guide and your navigation system.

Your inspiration, as you chart your journey forward.

Into the Light, so you can better see ahead of you.

Step by step, you will be empowered... and your path will be illuminated.

And don't worry about timeframes...

Everything happens when the time is right.

If you RUSH... to meet your "Imagined Deadlines"...

Then, the quality of the result will be compromised.

Take your Time.

Breathe and relax...

Imagine, zoom out, see your bigger picture, and then step forward into it!

At your own personal pace.

Time Management

You only have control over your OWN life, and how you choose to use your OWN time.

Use your Time as best you can, for we human beings are mortal...

Time is precious on the Earth Plane.

How we use our "Own Time"

What we do with our own personal Time is all about how we make choices.

How we steer our Lives along a path and head in a direction.

Most of us are uncertain of the "right" direction.

We are lacking a compass. So we look to our inner compass, and hope we aren't going to get "lost"...

We hold our Faith.

Faith in ourselves.

Freedom of Choice

As human kind, our views on the true power of our level of *"freedom"* are usually split somewhere between these two polarities.

1) *Some say our lives are already planned out for us, and that no matter what road we take, we are still headed for the same destination;*

2) *Others speculate that we have a great deal of power within us to choose our path and to aim towards a particular result or destination.*

The difference between these two views is the on-going debate of Fate Vs. Free Will.

Fate Vs. Free Will
This is a concept I have struggled with for a Lifetime.

Allow yourself to visualize a 30 centimeter ruler, like little people use at primary school.
As you stand in a point being 15 centimeters, this is recognized as "Now" on a chronological time scale. At zero centimeters, that point might represent "The Past"; and at 30 centimeters this position may be seen as "The Future".

As a Cancerian, on a personal level I tend to spend so much time projecting back to zero centimeters, or so much time worrying about 30 centimeters, that I am often finding that not enough of my real self, (my spirit or essence), is present enough – to be fully aware of what is occurring – in the 15 centimeter/NOW spot!

Past and Future
I believe that when you spend so much time thinking about the Past (that is clearly now gone), likewise while obsessing and worrying about the scary, unknown Future, you are actually projecting a component of your being, your energy: TO that zero or 30 centimeter point!

Living in "The NOW"
Because so much of yourself is there at either one of those points, and even at both, you seem to have a lighter grip on the reality of Now.

Your senses seem dulled, they aren't at maximum level. You may be functioning, like a machine would, but not really COMPLETELY AWARE of The Now. So, as a result, you miss half of it. While it's happening, you aren't really actively as present as you could've been. And then, before you know it, the Now starts to drift backwards until all of a sudden it's the Past, and it's gone before you had a chance to recognize its full potential.

Fate… is when the ruler keeps on moving, towards the zero mark. Things will keep on moving, they are fluid, ever-changing, by the will of the Universe.
This is Time.

Free Will…
Is when you are placed so firmly in your body, so firmly in the Now, that you can clearly see what's happening. Free will is when you quickly weigh up the Now situation, assess it fully, total up the Pro's and Con's of any action, recognize any opportunities that are presenting themselves to you, acknowledge any possible consequences of your actions, and realize that there will be *unknown* or *hidden* factors presenting themselves also.

Based upon all your quickly gathered knowledge, you then choose to act. You make a clear decision to act, and it's *your move* in the Universal Game of Life.

On top…
Consider this added into the equation:

As a Human Being…
You don't like the concept of possibly feeling like you are WASTING Time.

So that's hovering around in your mind as well.

Time... it keeps on ticking away.

The human dilemma.

Feeling "Stuck"

When Fear comes into play, you may find yourself to be "Stuck".

In Limbo-Land.

No-where Land. Afraid to get out of the quicksand because then you have to deal with the land-mines that are positioned all around, hidden underneath the ground. Reaching out for someone to pull you out of the quicksand, but no-one seems willing to help.

Maybe they're all afraid you might PULL THEM INTO THE QUICKSAND?!

You HAVE to get out.

You can do it.

If you REALLY WANT to.

Some people can spend YEARS in the quicksand, meanwhile...

Time moves on!

The Iris – A Flower Analogy...

Fate is like watching an Iris bloom. You don't know who planted the bulb.

That happened back at zero centimeters. You weren't even around then. But you say to yourself, it's been sunny, and there's been a bit of rain, so it looks like the bud is going to open.

You revere the Iris; you respect its beauty and uniqueness, so you choose to watch it open in its own little garden, in its own sense of Natural Time.

When it opens is its *own* business. But it will.

Free Will is like being at the 15 centimeter point on the Universal ruler.

As you walk along you see the Iris bud, growing.

You recognize its offering of beauty, so you pick it.

You choose it.

In picking the Iris's bud and taking it home, putting it in a vase, you are making it *yours*. Will it open, will it wilt? You do as much as you can for it, like putting it in water, trimming the stem, putting some of that Flower Life-Enhancing formula into the water, and you watch it every day.

But you have interfered in its Karma.

You have made it your business.

Sure, eventually it will bloom, have its prime, then eventually wilt and die.

At some stage as it moves on towards the 30 centimeter mark, you'll have to throw it away, give it back to Nature.

But you *chose* to pick it, so by your actions you effectively OWN part of it.

Because…

Once you make it yours -

It depends on *you*, for you have chosen to take some of the *responsibility* now, for its Fate.

You picked it, so unless you put it into a vase, it can no longer survive on its own.

It is no longer connected to Nature directly for its water and nutrients from the ground.

THINK BEFORE YOU CHOOSE.
THINK BEFORE YOU INTERFERE WITH NATURAL FLOW.

Also consider this:

As Time is passing, is the Iris moving towards the 30 centimeter mark, or the zero centimeter mark?

Is it moving into the Future, or into the Past?

Or both at once?

IS TIME LINEAR, LIKE A RULER?
OR IS TIME JUST A HUGE CIRCLE?
WITH NO ACTUAL BEGINNING, OR END?

DO WE EVER REALLY MOVE OFF ZERO POINT?

Or is Time simply an Illusion?
In the great scheme of things.

For the Heart,
Some say...
Time is ETERNAL.
Time = Infinity!

SENSES

Exploring the Senses

Our Senses are gauges.

They are flags, messages, they tell you about something. Often they are telling you things about yourself. Your likes, dislikes, does what you sense feel okay?

Listen to what your Senses are telling you – (and teaching you), about WHO you are and WHAT IS YOURS, & finding your true path and place in the world.

Here are some examples of how our senses work. What type of messages are they giving us about ourselves?

1. <u>Sight</u>: *Your eyes can see something so you know it's there. How does it look to you? Hmmm? Is it pretty? Colourful? Ugly? Dull? Shiny? Is it a car? A pair of shoes? A tree? No… you know it's a mail-box. A mail-box that's red & white, shaped like a miniature house.*
Message: I like red and white mailboxes, they look good to me.

2. <u>Taste</u>: *You can put something in your mouth and it either tastes good or not. It might be chocolate. Yum! You know the taste, and you like it a lot. You find it hard to eat only one piece. It tastes fantastic!*
Message: Chocolate tastes great, I really love it.

3. <u>Smell</u>: *You walk into a room and there is a vase of flowers there, you can smell the roses. They're pink. Your sight tells you that. But your nose tells you this – Mmmm… they smell good. Their perfume is incredible. They smell to you like the most heavenly of roses.*
Message: Things can "emote" beauty by more than one method. Not only are the roses beautiful to look at, but they also smell lovely. I remember smelling once such a beautiful smell when my first boyfriend gave me roses. Smell/scent is a strong memory trigger.

4. <u>Sound</u>: *You hear something. What's that sound? Ah yes, you know it's music. It is coming from the next door neighbour's house. Oh, I really love that song. It's one of my favourite songs. I know it because I've heard it heaps of times before.*

Message: That song is deeply stored in my memory and always triggers happy feelings within me. Sound is also a powerful memory trigger.

5. <u>Touch</u>: *Someone blind-folds you and takes you over to the other side of the room. They put your hand on something and say "What's that?" You feel it, stroke your hand over it. It's soft, fuzzy and warm. You can feel vibration through it too. It's a cat, it's purring.*

Message: I love cats, they feel so soft and they generate good feelings within me whenever I see one or touch its fur. I know it's happy because it's purring and that makes me feel content also.

Then... there is another sense.

Women are fully in touch with this sixth sense.
Males can practice getting familiar with it, because they DO possess it, but are generally not well practiced in using or understanding how it works, which is a pity....

OUR "SPOOKY" SENSE...

Knowing... but not really sure HOW we are knowing? But just KNOWING!

THE SIXTH SENSE

Our "Extra" Sense

Women have emotions.

They have them non-stop.
Emotions are with us women all the time.
We never get a break from them.

For women… it feels as natural as anything because we don't know any different. I've tried to explain to a man what it is like to be a woman.

This is the best example I can come up with:

Imagine a person talking on the phone –
(Yes - OK it *IS* probably going to be a woman….)
Ha-ha!
Or should I say… "LOL" ?
(Laugh out Loud)

But for the purpose of this example - it can be a person of either gender. When they are finished having their conversation they say goodbye and hang up the phone. When a person is watching a TV show, and the TV show is finished and they want to go to bed, then they turn off the TV. They pick up the remote control, say, and press "OFF". And the TV turns off.

The thing is… with this "other sense" it is *always* active. We cannot switch it off. We cannot hang it up. We are stuck there, connected to this "OPEN LINE" of communication that exists within the realm of our feelings. It is our gut, our being, our heart, our higher self, our connection with "Spirit", with "The Source" or "God", with "Angels", with "Guides" and the like.

It is our intuition, our gift of insight, our extra special sense. So, accepting that, who would want to tune it out or turn it off anyway? Isn't it better to be equipped with extra information about something?

When your other senses are dulled, it may be your strongest sense. It may be all we have to rely on when we are flying without a compass, trying to find our way in the dark, listening but not hearing anything helpful, or simply lost.

Even when we have the advantage of all of our other five senses working grandly for us, sometimes it is hard to ignore the "EXTRA" information we are being given.

Just like all the other senses, this extra sense tells us things about ourselves. Like the other five, our sixth sense gives us messages about ourselves, who we are, where we are headed, whether it feels right or wrong for us, bad or good for us, whether things "FIT" for us.

So, why males ignore these "emotions" I will never understand?! Why ignore useful information?
Okay... sure. It might feel uncomfortable or whatever, but if they only relaxed into the feeling it might help them answer valuable questions about themselves and help them steer their path through life a little clearer and/or sharper, with virtual ease.

THE OPEN LINE

8

"Tuning In" to the Universe

As I said before, women are RECEIVERS, but can also be *TRANSMITTERS*.

Men are generally TRANSMITTERS, but they can also be *RECEIVERS*.

Women are CONNECTED CONSTANTLY to the OPEN LINE OF EMOTIONS.

Keeping the line open is vital, women couldn't "hang up the line" or "turn it off", even if they wanted to. It's just always there.

Underlying.

Ever-present.

For a female, the "open line" is best described as...

A DIRECT LINE BETWEEN HERSELF AND THE UNIVERSE!

It is direct line hooked up between a woman's inner self and The Universe, to God and The Goddess, to a Higher Power, Deity, Intelligence both on the Earth Plane and the Celestial Heavens... a direct line of a concentrated light beam connected deeply at her end into her soul, the other end just like a radar in space, picking up infinite frequencies. She must learn to recognize the frequencies emitting.

A woman must become sensitive to her received transmissions. If you like, from space, or wherever, some from people on the Earth, in any case, she must learn the art of discrimination.

She must learn to filter them, to decipher their codes, to recognize that they are from Love and Light, and to disregard, ignore and reject all else and otherwise.

That is what is known as emotion:
Receiving transmission.

From one's own soul, from the environment, your surroundings, your friends and family, people you meet, and those around that are unseen yet there. From Angels, Guides, Helpers, Teachers, Ancestors. Transmission from the Cosmos.

It's like surfing the net without logging on.
It's like talking on the phone without dialing.

Global transmission...
Welcome on-line, Cosmic Spirit!

LIGHT

9

The Magic of Colour & Light

Light.
Colours occur ... because of Light.

All colours are made up out of light and represent an area of the white
light spectrum.

Each colour is unique in that what it represents is its own individual frequency. Each colour radiates and illustrates our lives on planet Earth. Each colour is beautiful in its own right and has its own realm of possibility attached to it.

Every colour and shade is relevant in the sacred rainbow of Life.

We all remember the old school-day experiment where we discovered in Science class that the colours of the rainbow are made up of white light bent or "refracted" through a glass or crystal prism.

From a single white light beam the light is bent and exits the clear prism spread perfectly into a spectrum of colour. The colour bands sit alongside each other in perfect harmony, like stripes, each different... yet belonging to the same family of white light.

Colours are all part of the One yet unique to themselves, colours are so individual yet part of us all. Race, creed, colour, we human-folk are all one and the same. We are all souls that make up the one, that being the Universe.

So, let's celebrate the colours of life and explore them further. Let us meditate upon each individual meaning and symbolism. Colours lend their own special energies to certain areas of the life experience.

Colour and light are ever-present and constant, even when it cannot be seen by the naked eye.

Today, everywhere, Light is used to transmit, receive and store information.

Light Speed

"Light Speed..." whispered Lady Guinevere to her cherished Arthur and her beloved Lancelot, as the brave King and his Knights set off together, upon their Quest.

So what *IS* Light Speed?

Light travels at a speed of approximately 376,000 miles per hour.

Some people speculate that if we humans could find a method to travel at the speed of light, then "time" as we know it would cease to exist, for we could travel at equal speed.

Time Travel

If we could travel faster than the speed of light, we could travel backwards in time, as well as into the future. Time travel has always been a fascination of ours, human kind, that is. If there is a way to cheat time, I would imagine it involves travel via means of the use of Light.

Audio and Video Files

Music can be stored on CD's and played by laser beams of Light. Video/Graphics files can also be stored on CD/DVD and played using a light beam which "reads" the data stored. Light is used everywhere to send and transmit voice, sound and pictures.

Optical Fibers

The miracle of Optical Fiber Technology breaks down the speaker's voice into coded information and transmits the information to another part of the world in the form of a light beam. Upon receipt at the other end, the light is de-encrypted back into its original sound and the person on the other end hears it exactly as it was spoken. A single optical fiber can hold up to 90,000 calls at one time. So this one conversation can travel by light, still allowing 89,999 other conversations to share the same light beam.

Ultra Violet

If we think we might be looking a bit pale and the winter seems to be dragging on forever, then we can go into the solarium and get a faster suntan, via the use of special light globes that emit certain types of concentrated rays. Ultra-violet light is used in solariums; it originates from the Violet/Indigo section of the light spectrum.

Infra Red

Infra-red, which comes from the Red/Yellow section of the light spectrum, is used in modern-day heating. It is also more recently used in a concentrated laser beam to transmit pictures over short range. The latest mobile telephones and handheld "Palm Pilot" units – (ie: small computers that can be held in the hand and retail for a few hundred dollars in the stores) feature this technology.

You don't have to "Text" or "PXT" using the SMS system anymore, if the recipient is within a few hundred metres you can infra-red beam the picture or file over to them, without "paying" for it to go through the telephone network. Infra-red has a close "cousin" in the spectrum called Red/Yellow which produces more incandescent light.

BLUETOOTH... IS YET A NEWER DEVELOPMENT STILL...

Based on the same transmission basis... (ie: find device, or detect - and share data files...) principles as Infra-Red, but by using a cooler end of the colour spectrum (BLUE) - to transmit the data.

Frequencies of Colour

So, the different colour beams to be found within the spectrum are quite different, produce different rays of light, and can be used for different purposes.

Different colours travel at different speeds and their frequency differs by the type of 'wave" produced. They have their own separate vibration; therefore each colour of the spectrum can be associated to a particular quality of energy, not unlike a "feeling" or "emotion".

Love and light are inseparable twins.

Where there is Love
There is Light.

Where there is Light
There is Love.

Let's think of them as the original founders of a corporation:
Let's call it…

"Love & Light Incorporated…."

Love & Light Inc.

L&L Inc.

Colouring our Lives on Earth.

IMAGINE THE COLOUR WHEEL:

Yellow, Orange, Red, Red/Violet are in the WARMER end of the spectrum.

While...

Violet, Blue, Green, then back to Yellow, are in the COOLER end of the spectrum.

Imagine the spectrum as a GIANT WHEEL...

Or:

360 degrees.

AN ENDLESS CIRCLE OF COLOUR FREQUENCIES.

Without end... eternal...

Like the Circle of Life.

Which encompasses and colours our Life experiences.

THE RAINBOW SPECTRUM

What the different colour frequencies represent

The basic colours of the spectrum are detailed here, but every other colour, shade or nuance fall somewhere inside or between these basic colour categories, as they are made up of "blends" of colour.

RED   Strength, passion, vitality, power, sexuality, intensity;

YELLOW   Intellect, thoughts and ideas, clarity, focus,
            communication;

PINK   Love: (in its purest form), happiness, calm, softness;

GREEN   Growth, prosperity, wealth, good luck, development;

PURPLE   Spirituality, faith, belief, healing, royalty, magic and mystery;

ORANGE   Vitality, higher energy, vibrancy, optimism, enthusiasm;

BLUE   Healing, repair, renewal, peace, calm, tranquility, rejuvenation;

WHITE   Absolute Love & Light!
             Peace, Positivity, Purity.
             WHITE is all colour combined:
             The highest form of Light.

BLACK   It is important to note that BLACK is not a colour at all!
             Black has NO LIGHT.

Black is the total absence of light, it is the negative/opposite of Light.

Two other important "elemental" colours are:

GOLD   Sun/solar energy, strong masculine energy. Strength, wealth, success;

SILVER   Moon/astral energy, softer feminine energy, compassion, nurturing.

These two metallic colours represent the two best known semi-precious and precious minerals that are found within the Earth. They occur naturally in nature. But they also have an affinity with the masculine and feminine energies.

Light is always there, whether you can see it or not. Light is energy.

A Colour... is a concentrated and unique frequency of the light spectrum.

Rainbows... Nature's Gift to Humanity.
They are pretty spectacular.
People ALWAYS stop...and gasp in delight!
And point EXCITEDLY at them as they magically appear in the sky after or during a sprinkle of rain on a sunny day.

From children, to adults, we ALL adore a rainbow!
Breathtaking evidence of...
Heaven on Earth.

See next page - Table:" Colour Vibrations & Energies"

<u>Colour:</u>	<u>Symbol:</u>	<u>Keywords:</u>
RED	⚡	*Passion/Intensity*
YELLOW	📖	*Intellect/Mind*
PINK	♥	*Love/Happiness*
GREEN	$	*Growth/Prosperity*
PURPLE	☯	*Spirituality/Mystery*
ORANGE	☼	*Vitality/Enthusiasm*
BLUE	✞	*Healing/Tranquility*
WHITE	★	*Light/Source*
GOLD	♂	*Solar/Masculine*
SILVER	♀	*Lunar/Feminine*

QUARTZ CRYSTALS

Natures Energy Transmitters & Receivers

Quartz Crystals occur naturally.

They are found within the Earth and usually are housed within the centre of hollow rocks and boulders. They are formulated over a process of time, which can be tens, hundreds, or even thousands of years.

Their special "housing" rocks are called "Geodes".

How are Quartz Crystals "made"?
Similar to stalactites and stalagmites, Quartz is formed and grows within caves or underground. Quartz are derived of the concentrated mineral deposits found everywhere in the Earth, and these are responsible for the formulation of their individual colour and variety.

They are extracted from the Earth, just like Gold or Silver, which are also made naturally out of minerals.

The same elements of nature are found to be present within the better-known varieties of gemstones or precious metals, and Quartz is made the same way. Precious gems, gold and silver, are highly prized and valued in a material market, but Quartz is not as highly regarded in terms of financial value.

In monetary terms Quartz is less precious, but its "value" and merit is highly regarded and recognized in other forms- (ie: the spiritual "properties" of the Quartz).

The crystals occur in many colours and varieties, and can be either natural, rough, as they are when first cut out of their rocks, or polished and tumbled into smoother specimens.

Whether they are smooth or rough, Quartz Crystals are special. The aesthetic value is valid, as they are extremely beautiful, but the true power is to be found within the crystals individual properties.

Many are found in the mines in South America, but Quartz is found all over the world.

Some Quartz varieties are the result of volcanic lava eruptions, hot as molten lava, then cooled and solidified within rock, over extensive Time.

They can grow as individual entities, or they can occur en-masse, in cluster formation.

Quartz has its own special quality of being able to absorb, store and also release "Energy".

Today watches are powered by quartz, but we can use them ourselves within our home and environment to encourage Love and Light, harmony, and to effect positive change in our lives.

Crystal Power
The crystal's power resides in both its *COLOUR* and the *ENERGY* associated to that particular variety.

Crystals can be used to assist in Affirmation and Visualization, due to their specific properties and affinity with certain aspects of the Life Experience.

As we learned about the Power of Colours previously, we can apply the "Colour Rule" to this concept. Whatever effect you may be hoping to achieve, whatever you may need help with, there is a particular crystal which can best assist you with your development.

Keeping a tumbled stone with you, on your person, in your pocket or in your home can be very beneficial.

It will help to bring that quality you seek to harness much closer to you, and help you better align yourself with its vibration.

Varieties and Colours

There are many varieties of Quartz and, but I will outline here the better known varieties, each one corresponding with an Energy type, or frequency as represented in the Colour Spectrum discussed earlier.

I've included Gold and Silver also – (although they are both precious mineral elements), because they too have a powerful affinity with certain types of Energy.

For Meditation:

It may not be very far away in the future until all of our data…
Our precious collection of information, memories and moments –
Might be stored globally – perhaps even Universally?…

WITHIN QUARTZ CRYSTAL!

Instead of today's presently used methods of Hard Drives, USB Sticks, DVD/ CD's.

We will explore" Data Storage" in Quartz here shortly… using the ANCIENT method.
By Programming and Accessing – by means via the power of Heart and Mind.

Table: "Quartz Crystal Energies"

Varieties:	Colour:	Qualities:	Symbol:
Bloodstone / Garnet	Red	Passion/Strength	⚡
Amber / Citrine	Yellow	Communication/Ideas	📖
Rose Quartz	Pink	Love/Happiness	♥
Jade / Green Obsidian	Green	Growth/Prosperity	$
Amethyst	Purple	Spirituality/Healing	☯
Tiger Eye / Agate	Orange	Vitality/Spirit	☼
Lapis Lazuli / Turquoise	Blue	Healing/Protection	✝
Clear Quartz / Apophyllite	White	Magnification /Concentration	★
Gold	Gold	Solar/Masculine	♂
Silver	Silver	Lunar/Feminine	♀

Programming & Accessing

We know that Quartz is both a *Receiver and Transmitter of Energy*. It can also store or "house" energy for later use.

The specific energy of the crystal can be further "boosted" by "programming" your crystal with your own thoughts.

Programming Your Crystal – ("Transmitting")

When you wish to Program your crystal, you must hold it in your RIGHT hand. Your RIGHT hand is your PROJECTIVE hand. It is controlled by one side of your brain that being the hemisphere of the brain which relates to "mechanical action, performing tasks, practical use." That's why a lot of people write and perform very strongly with their right hand.

Whilst holding it, send it happy thoughts through your mind, through your body, and through your spirit. Send your energy flowing into the crystal and "fill it up" with the type of energy that it is designed to be a receptacle for.

For example, if it is a Rose Quartz, send it thought and feelings of love and happiness. These feelings will be stored in the "Heart" of the crystal, for when you need a bit extra of that type of energy in your life. The crystal "records" your thoughts and stores the vibrations within itself.

Accessing Your Crystal – ("Receiving")

When you wish to Access your crystal, you must hold it in your LEFT hand. Your left hand is your RECEPTIVE hand. It is controlled by the other side of your brain that being the hemisphere of the brain which relates to "imagination, dreams, memories, creativity, inspiration."

Whilst holding it, in your LEFT hand, you can feel the crystal becoming warm and releasing slowly the previously stored energy into your system. As it releases energy into your body, you can draw upon it at times when you are feeling depleted of such energy.

For example, if it's a Rose Quartz and you are feeling a bit down and sad, draw the Love and Happiness energy from your crystal and feel it boost your own emotional state of mind.

Filtering Energy
One other thing, as it's giving you the GOOD energy, it is actually DRAWING your negativity out of you, like sponge absorbing dirty water.

That's why it's important to cleanse your crystals once in a while. It sends out positivity whilst FILTERING negativity from your "system" and Spirit.

Cleansing
Cleansing can be done whenever you feel the crystal needs a little bit of a renewal or a boost. That way it can be filtered of its negativity, and recharged freshly to work more efficiently.

Cleansing can be done once a month, on the night of the Full Moon. This is because the Moon at this time has a very powerful yet gentle and feminine energy, conducive to soothing, renewing, and re-charging. It is best to place your crystals in a glass or ceramic basin, or bowl of water, and a bit of rock salt wouldn't go astray either. Sea salt is best, for it represents the ocean and its cleansing capacity. We all know that salt water is nature's version of an antiseptic.

Place your crystal(s) outside under the beams of light coming from the moon-rays, and let the moonlight charge up the water and revitalize your little "friends".

They'll love it.

The Essential Trilogy

Rose Quartz, Clear Quartz and Amethyst are the MUST HAVE crystal combination. Together these make up a special ***trilogy of power***, but each of these three forms can be individually and potently powerful in their own right.

Rose Quartz – "The Love Stone"

Rose Quartz is one of the most beautiful types of quartz available. This is because it holds within it the power to energize the Heart Chakra to Love, bringing Love and Happiness into the heart of the holder.

There are many types of Love, but the Rose Quartz ensures that all and every type of Love is encouraged and shall be developed within the life of the holder.

It is said that there is no greater Love than that which is directed inwards towards one's self...

So - for anybody to be able to truly Love another ...
They must first fully come to know Love for and within themselves.

For A Broken Heart

If there has been upset or disappointment in Love, should you require the healing of a broken heart, or should they find or feel that Love is lacking within your life, then this is the variety of Quartz you *must* have.

It should be placed near you, for example:

Where you sleep, where you spend a lot of time, in your pocket, worn upon your body. Especially a heart-shaped specimen, worn over the Heart Charka as a pendant, or simply a tumbled piece kept on your person, within your Aura – (eg: like in your pocket).

Rose Quartz encourages the presence of:

Pure Love, Self-Love, Romantic Love, Harmony, Calm, Healing, Relationships...

Forgiveness, Compassion, Love – (Unconditional Love), Friendship, Fertility, Trust, Acceptance.

It clears stored negativity, dispels anger, resentment and jealousy. It can help to bring upon greater feelings of self worth and confidence.

A Special Blessing
Rose Quartz may bestow upon us the gift of assisting the development of greater Love towards our own self. Therefore, the natural process of formulating loving relationships with others can be... similarly to tending a precious seedling: "Sewn, Grown, and Known".

Amethyst – "The Spiritual Healer"
Amethyst, due to its purple hue, is related to spirituality and the strong energy of healing.

It helps with healing not only on a physical level but on an emotional and spiritual level. It heals the Soul. This is why it is so powerful, because at the root of any disease is an unresolved matter of the Spirit. Holding onto past hurts or negative feelings can often manifest as illness later on.

That's why Amethyst is so potent in its healing ability. It gets to the cause of the matter, and helps to dissolve the negativity.

You will notice your cluster of Amethyst can change colour due to the amount of negativity it has absorbed from its environment. It works like a filter, so it needs to be cleansed regularly.

Amethyst has a gentle energy, like that of a nurse, so it is advisable to keep it near your sleeping place. If you are suffering from insomnia, anxiety or sleeplessness, if you should be experiencing bad dreams or difficulty in "winding down" and relaxing, then this is the variety of quartz that you need.
PURPLE...

Magic, Mystery and Majesty
Amethyst also helps to increase your powers of intuition because it has an affinity with all matters spiritual and magical. It may help you to find more restful sleep, and aid you in understanding the symbolism of your dream interpretations.

Amethyst is also connected with Majesty, for centuries it has been found to be set in royal crowns/head-dresses. This is because purple is traditionally associated with royalty and it offers a gift of protection to the wearer.

Clear Quartz – "The Magnifying Glass"
Clear Quartz is an energy "booster".
Rest assured, it's definitely Quartz, - (NOT glass), but you should think about it in this way...

It's like a magnifying glass.

It concentrates and strengthens the energy for you. It particularly relates to mental clarity and focus, therefore it helps you think and be mentally agile. It is best avoided near a sleeping place as it can actually PROMOTE sleeplessness. It may stimulate your mind so much that you cannot relax.

That is why it is advisable to keep Clear quartz out of the bedroom, but instead keep in your office, or anywhere where you have to think a lot. It helps you to come up with ideas, it encourages clearer written or verbal communication, and it helps you solve problems. It is a concentrator, stimulator and magnifier of *THOUGHT*.

Combining Quartz Varieties

If you should use Clear Quartz with another type of Quartz, it will *magnify* the properties of the other piece.

So, if you are using Clear Quartz next to a cluster of Amethyst, for example, then the Healing Energy of the Amethyst will be *strengthened considerably*.

Remember: Adding Clear Quartz to any "combination" gives the other types of Quartz magnification and extra intensity. It energises them.

There are many other varieties of Quartz as I presented earlier, but these three are probably the most popular, most "effective" and most widely used types.

Indeed, they make up a special *"Trilogy of Power"* when used or placed together.

Think about it…
What type of result do you think would be generated?

$$\blacktriangledown + \odot + \bigstar = ?$$

ESTABLISHING A DIALOUGUE

Exploring your relationship with The Universe

This Universe we are part of... is WONDROUS.

ABUNDANT and SPECTACULAR.

Ask the Universe for what you want.

Imagine the Universe as an all-seeing, all-knowing, beautiful, loving and compassionate, incredible realm of endless possibility.

Imagine it...
As it is.

SEE IT ALL AROUND YOU... "LOVE & LIGHT INC."

Light Workers
At the heart-centre of activity... exists a strong network of "Light Workers".

Imagine it as being a giant corporation... L& L Inc.
Maybe YOU work there too?

To assist you in your work there are many others working there, some more advanced in their "spiritual career" and some still in training – (like *you*).

Imagine when you had a problem in your daily working task.

You've been over it and over it and you can't seem to get on top of the problem.

What would you do? You've been to your superiors and they seem to be stuck as well. You've asked everyone on your floor and they are all equally stumped for answers.

So, what would you do?
How can you solve this problem?
This is where dialogue with the Universe comes in.
Some call it "Prayer".

In any case, it's about asking for help.

But how?

There are a set of rules that you must acknowledge when you are asking for help.

Asking the Universe for Help

Keeping calm, centred and positive ensures you message will be heard clearly and understood perfectly. Keep it positive, be completely focused and clear.

You would expect your issue to be well received if you are calm and clear.

The Managing Director and/or Chief Executive Officer of the "Love & Light Corporation" are more likely to listen and co-operate if you approach the "meeting" in a well prepared state.

If you went into a Board Meeting and started crying or screaming hysterically, the Directors and Senior Executives would quickly grow impatient with your behaviour. Furthermore, they would find themselves totally unable to understand your problem or request.

So, work out the nature of your problem and prepare to present it to the Board of the Love and Light Corporation. You are about to enter into a Dialogue with Source.

ASKING FOR HELP

13

Call a "Board Meeting"

You might like to blow a dandelion into the wind...
But there are other ways to make a wish.

Imagine a Board Meeting.

Who might attend such a meeting? Give it some thought.

Love & Light Inc.

At the Love and Light Corporation there are never any apologies, everyone is in attendance. Just because you can't see the attendees doesn't mean they aren't listening. Just like Light, sometimes you cannot see it, but it may be all around you at any given moment.

When you enter your Boardroom mentally, you are preparing to pray.
When you "pray"… or "ask"… or "affirm"…
Imagine that you are addressing the Board.

All others agenda's are irrelevant at this meeting.
It's a very private meeting, set up ONLY at **YOUR** request.
You don't have to check diaries or fit in with schedules, you can hold such a meeting whenever you feel it's required.

The important thing is to relax, centre yourself; you may close your eyes if you wish. You may be sitting, lying down, waiting for a bus, walking in the park…

As long as you have a few moments to yourself, where you are able to relax your mind.

In your mind's eye, visualize a certain group of individuals, those parties to whom you wish to direct your request.

Addressing the Board

I firstly like to address the group with respect, for I know these individuals have absolutely earned their positions on the Board; they are well qualified for the task.

I usually begin…

"Dear Universe, God, Angels, Helpers, Spirits, Guides, Teachers, Ancestors…
All that is Love and Light,"

I then begin my personal dialogue and explain to them what my problems or requests are.

I try to be as specific as possible… as clear as I can be, about what I need from them to help my situation.

I may ask for safety, good health, protection, happiness, peace of mind, or anything.

These are some indicators…

If I am ill, I ask for healing.

If I am confused, I ask for clarity.

If I am tired, I ask for rest and the ability for greater concentration.

If I am sad, I ask for happiness.

It could be about money, or other more material concerns…
After all, this IS a material world of form we live in.
Money is not everything.
But without it on this Earth plane, we could perish.
It is the currency of humanity - that sustains us.

We need to be realistic...

Without money – Life can be difficult here.

Many of us stress over bills and finances.

It is part of the Human Experience.

Sometimes there seems to be more going out than coming in.

And this causes many of us worry and can affect our health.

Trust that the Universe is listening and aware...

And ASK...

If you need help.

Sometimes when you ask...

You receive MORE than you ever initially expected.

If I am struggling to pay bills, I ask for help to achieve greater financial freedom.

If you ask for help, you will receive it.

Company Policy

At L&L Inc. there is a strong policy in place that applies to everyone.

That policy states:

"WE CAN OBSERVE, BUT WE CANNOT INTERFERE IN OTHER PEOPLE'S LIVES. EVERYONE COMES TO PLANET EARTH WITH FREE WILL. FREEDOM OF CHOICE...

INTERFERING EQUATES TO DISRESPECTING AN INDIVIDUAL'S POWER OF FREE WILL. IT IS INTERFERING WITH THEIR KARMA. WE CAN, HOWEVER, ASSIST IF WE ARE ASKED TO ASSIST. BUT ONLY WHEN ASKED!"

Everyone at L&L Inc. adheres strictly to this policy.

In a way, it would be good if human beings could respect it also.

Exceptions to... The Rule:
Of course, there are some occasions when an individual may be too little or too ill to be able to ask, like an infant who is unwell for example. In this case it is often the parents or loved one's who may ask for help on the child's behalf.

The request *will* of course be heard, but the Board will ultimately determine whether or not the child be spared from its personal Karma.

Equilibrium Preservation
There is a special "equilibrium preservation" rule relating to matters of Karma.

That rule works like this:

"When you try to prevent a human being from fulfilling their own personal Karma, you may be successful in "removing" their "Karmic Challenge"...

But, to "balance" the equation, YOU may actually inherit that Karma for yourself."

A Positive Affirmation

"Of all the gifts life has to offer
Many are subtly wrapped in disguise
Some are draped in glitz and glamour
Others more difficult to recognise

What may seem a mere chance meeting
May well blossom into new togetherness
Nurtured along like a precious bonsai
Tended and shaped with great finesse

The gift of a heart that's given freely
Is one that sustains through joy and tears
Empowering those who share in the gift
Developing deeper throughout many years

The universe in all its grandeur
Presents before us various lessons
All may be courageously overcome
It met headlong with strength of essence

Draw from pure love the power needed
An endless well within ones soul
Build upon the depth of character
Required to reach our one true goal."

KARMA

14

Cause and Effect

The Law of Karma is simple and exact.
Precise!

What you do comes back.
What you plant you will see grow.
What you do to others will come back to you.
A kindness will result in an unexpected kindness... and so forth.

But, if you should introduce any negativity into your intent, remember, what you do/wish/say/think will come back to you THREEFOLD.

That is... *three times stronger.*

That is why it is vital to act positively and keep your thoughts and spoken words absolutely positive. Be ever-mindful of your thoughts as they are powerful.
Spoken word is powerful and action is the ultimate power.

Karma is specifically... the rule of CAUSE and EFFECT.
For every ACTION there is an opposite RE-ACTION or RESULT.
When you ask the Universe for something, you are keeping it very personal, and you are mainly anticipating a result which will affect YOU.

However, remember that the Universe will tailor the result to you, yet in doing so; it *WILL* affect other people's situations, even if only a little.

Sometimes, it might affect them a lot.

For example, if you are in an unsatisfactory relationship and you wish to attract a more appropriate partner into your life, you may ask the Universe to send you what would be your ideal partner.

Let's imagine such a scenario:

"Bring them to me, oh Universe. Send me Mr Wonderful (or Miss Perfect); he/she should be this and this and this and this... He/she should have the qualities of – (insert qualities)...

Send him/her to me soon please, so that we can meet and can be blissfully happy and fulfilled and live happily ever after – blah blah blah…"

The "To Do" Basket
So, your request is in.
In the TO DO BASKET.
Getting handled by the Team.

A few months later, your current partner comes home and tells you that he is in love with his secretary and he's moving out. Oh well, you decide that's okay… *Kind* of!

You aren't that worried because you already knew things weren't shaping up to be ideal, otherwise you wouldn't be asking the Universe to send you someone more suitable.

However, it does come as a bit of a shock. You didn't expect it to be this way. Her? You can't believe it! You never saw it coming.

Details… Details… Details
When you asked the Universe to send you the ideal person, which was as simply as you put it.
Nothing more.
You kept it simple.

The Universe certainly can and usually will take care of your request, but there are many other factors that the "Universal Team" has got to take care of.

Fine tuning the plan, you know… (all the "behind the scenes" stuff).
Details.

Other "players" in the drama.

The Universe never sees things as *"that simple"*.

So, of course, The Universe has worked things out quite thoroughly. The Universe is preparing to set up a "chance meeting" for you and Mr/Miss Mysterious.

But it further takes into account that your *current* partner will have to receive a *balanced* action, maybe someone for *them* to love, so that there's some kind of equilibrium.

You may not exactly like what is now happening, but indirectly, you asked for it.

The Universe just goes that **little bit further** in creating a balanced effect, all around.

No detail goes unnoticed.
You must very carefully think about the possible repercussions of your request, should it be granted. Imagine the possible results.

Because... **WORDS ARE POWERFUL.**

With Power comes Responsibility.
When exercising your Power of Free Will, bear ever-present in mind that exact rule. Power DEMANDS Responsibility.

The entire Universe and all present within it, can feel the effects, of a single private "Wish" or "Command."

Be careful what you wish for, as the old saying says, because you might just get it.

Remember...

"Plant the seed —
It will grow
But be very careful of what you plant...
Ensure... that it's not a weed!"

The Universe is always acting in the interests of the HIGHEST GOOD... for all concerned.

But by planting a seed - you are PERSONALLY taking responsibility for the result.

For everything in the Universe, there is ALWAYS an "opposite/ negative" mirror, or reaction...

So, ensure you keep it POSITIVE!

Many of us ask for things in our mind -
That REALLY... if we GET 100% SERIOUS about it...
WE DO NOT REALLY WANT AT ALL!

So, be serious in your thoughts and intentions... yet keep it light.

BE KIND TO OTHERS.

BE KIND TO YOURSELF.

Think CAREFULLY - about what you *REALLY* want.

Fantasy...
Is the VERY first step - in the process of Creation.

The Necessary Halves

"XY and XX, Youth and Maiden
Man and Woman, He and She
Adam and Eve, Yin and Yang
Negative and Positive, Land and Sea;

Sun and Moon, Sturdy and Serene
Strong and Frail, King and Queen
Violence and Compassion, Black and White
Harsh and Sensitive, Day and Night;

God and Goddess, Father and Mother
Son and Daughter, Seducer and Lover
War and Peace, Destruction and Re-birth
Sorrow and Joy, Insecurity and Self-worth."

ASKING THE UNIVERSE

15

Prayer & Affirmation

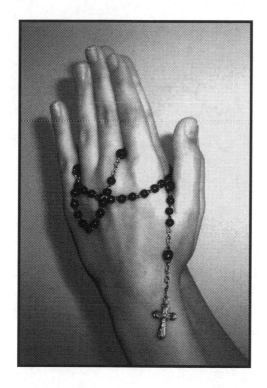

When you ask, you pray, or you affirm...

You are asking for help - in achieving a result.

YOU ARE MAKING AN ANNOUNCEMENT OVER THE L&L NETWORK.
YOU ARE SUMMONING GOD & THE ANGELS INTO ACTION.

You are requesting: "Manifestation of your hearts deepest desires…"

YOU ARE LOGGING ON AND SENDING YOUR ORDER INTO CYBERSPACE.

The result will be given.

Your answer, your *"wish"* can be powerfully manifest.
If you fuel it with your most powerfully concentrated energy…

Derived of your inner-most "Feelings & Emotions".

But you must be aware of The Rules.

Prayer –
When making a prayer…
Focus, relax and be clear in your idea and your communication of it.

THE RULES:
These are "The GENERAL Rules…"
When having a Prayer Dialogue with the Board of L&L Inc.

There is no STRICT HEAVY PENALTY FOR NOT STICKING TO IT.

IT IS JUST A GUIDELINE, TO KEEP THINGS EASY AND IN PERSPECTIVE.

120

Prayer needn't been heavily laden with anguish and urgency.
The message will always get through.
You don't need to shout, weep, or take out a full page ad!
Prayer is not a flashing neon-lit billboard, screaming its point to the city.
It is a quiet, introspective, serene time.

1. NO Hysteria! Be cool, calm and collected. Try to stay rational - even if it is a highly emotionally charged issue. By staying grounded you will be able to see the circumstances more objectively... and then can present the issue forward with greater focus and attention to detail. The sharper the information you can put forward, the more crystal-clear it will be received.

2. Don't bother yourself with trying to HELP "them" to come up with a solution. Simply trust in the fact that they know what they are doing and it will be handled by the best. Have absolute faith that it will be worked out for you and you *will* be shown or given a solution or result, when the time is appropriate.

3. Don't burst a brain cell about time-frames. Remember that these are extremely busy "people" who receive countless requests; they will put your request into their ENORMOUS "TO DO" basket ...and get to solving your problem as soon as they can. There are a TEAM of "people and individuals" working for L&L Inc. They've got their best people onto it behind the scenes, rest assured. You will get an answer or result, as soon as is practically possible.

4. Always thank the Board for listening and helping. Yes...they're very busy "people" - but they always seem to find or make the time to hear your problems. Simply hold your faith... while you are anticipating your response.

5. Respect and obey the Law of Karma. Only ask for things which YOU need. Don't try to control anyone else's life! It can only result in BAD Karma.

6. When you have ended your dialogue - always remember to remain "OPEN" to receiving solutions. By remaining "open" you are not limiting yourself. You will learn to keep your "antennae" active in whatever you do in your day to day life. If you go to the shops, or go to perform errands… be open to whom you might meet. They could have a "special" message for you which may just contain "The Answer". You may hear a song on the radio? Or see a street sign? Even a conversation you may overhear in the street… may bless you - by giving you some vital clue to your being able to solve your problem.

7. A little Tip! Don't demand a specific solution. Give the Universe a "guideline" but be open in receiving something similar. If you say you want only "a little bit of money" you may get "only a little bit of money". Be mindful of your exact wording. Forget about feeling "greedy", it's an endless sea of resources out there.

8. In your request, maintain a high impression of your level of deservingness, have a high standard of your vision of self-worth. For example: If you want a new car, don't limit your scope by specifically asking for a specific car… because to your delight, the Universe might actually think you deserve a Mercedes Benz! Remember: More than you EVER could imagine or expect… IS possible. More than you think you deserve! So just say instead, "I really need a new car." Trust in the Universe/Source that you will receive what is exactly correct and perfect for you. After all, they know you through and through at L&L Inc.

The FAMILY of L&L Inc. knows precisely… what suits you best.
You've been working with them all your life.
(Maybe even other life-times?!)
So, it is natural to accept - that they DO know you pretty well by now!

"BE OPEN TO RECEIVING!"

Open your Heart and Mind to endless possibilities and outcomes.

Don't be upset if you don't receive exactly what you want.
Because you will receive something - ideal for you.

It may be something even better than what you could've ever dreamed of.

Meet the Board Members:

The Universe	All that is! The Universe… Source, Light, Love, Cosmic Spirit, Infinity.
God	Your personal version of "God". A Figurehead, God/Goddess, Deity, whatever your religion or belief is, your vision/idea of "God" is unique. Maybe for some… The Universe and God are One and the same? There's no right or wrong about it… No-one else's version of "God" is any different, any better or worse, than any other's personal version of God.
Angels	A network of Angels who consist of Guardian Angels, Arch Angels, both on Earth and in the Celestial Realms.

Helpers	They may be Angelic or they may exist on the Earth Plane, sent here to perform tasks of assistance. They may be in human form, perhaps someone you may know or encounter. Someone you might have the opportunity to meet with. On Earth they may be human beings, such as: Nurses, counselors, friends, artists, fire-men, police-men, and doctors, anyone working in a compassionate and service role.
Spirits/Guides	They may be energies around you that are sent to steer you in the right path that is truest for you.
Teachers	May be on this Earth or otherwise, all those who can teach us something valuable to better equip us to make wise choices in our life's journey. Teachers are well learned in their area of expertise and are available to share their knowledge and wisdom with others who ask.
Ancestors	Some of us may have a strong feeling of relationship with ancestors that were around in the past but have since passed over. It could be a grandparent or relative that you may have been particularly close to. If this is the case you will sense when they are close by recognizing a familiar, warm energy of love and protection. There are many ancestors in spirit from your lineage; in any case they shared the same human element of inherited genetic material, and of spirit. They know who *you* are, whether you have met them or not, because they were responsible for you being in existence. Ancestors are loyal protectors of "their own".

Personal Power

"The power
The strength
Of the uttered word
Far greater
Indeed larger
Than man may observe

Yet almost
As weighty
Are thoughts unheard
For thoughts too
Are things
Shall the cosmos serve

A single command
Is there substance
In that?
The deepest, most private
And intimate dream

A desire
Like a wish
Either conjured or spat
A verbal request
May enhance your Fates theme

A notion
Quite tiny
The faintest idea

A whim
A mere inkling
May manifest clear

The force
In ourselves
This mystical means
Is often
The player
Behind the scenes."

LIGHT AND THE ANGELS

16

Love & Light Incorporated

Here's another way of looking at the "Board" members at the meeting.

I've put together some position descriptions for the "L&L Inc." Board Meeting.

The Universe: *The Source – Love & Light.*

God: *Managing Director/ Chief Executive Officer*

Angels: *Directors & Senior Executives – (Decisive action)*

Helpers: *Personal Assistants to the Directors/Executives*

Spirits/Guides: *Individual Staff Mentors*

Teachers: *Department of Training and Human Resources*

Ancestors: *Advisors/Consultants...*
Now long retired, but still well respected for their experience...
OR – Those who worked there and retired - perhaps LONG before you ever existed.

A WORD ABOUT GOD...

Like most big corporations, other than the Board Meetings, not many people have a lot to do with the Managing Director or Chief Executive Officer. He's usually INCREDIBLY busy, jetting about to foreign countries or exotic destinations, and may turn up in the office only once in a blue moon.

Some people who work for him don't even know what he LOOKS like, they never see him. His Time is highly valuable; he attends important meetings all over the Globe. He's in demand!

God, like the MD or CEO, employs many "others" to take care of the actual workings of the organization. He just kind of "oversees" everything and makes the REALLY huge decisions. He's a *very* busy person.

So, God has his staff efficiently taking care of the more practical details on his behalf. Sometimes, he sits there and works out an extensive plan with his fellow "Directors" and "Executives", but he then leaves it up to them to deploy the actual plan of action.

Of course, they also have others to assist them in undertaking the activity. So, like I explained earlier, there's a whole network of "staff" both in Spirit and on the Earth Plane, that take care of business.

About Angels

Angels are pretty busy!

But because they aren't always on the Earth Plane they need to get onto Earth somehow, to help distribute the instructions among the human element of "staff".

To do this they need Light.

Why Angels Love Light

Angels travel along Light.

They dwell in Light therefore they are most comfortable being within Light. They find it difficult to reach us and help us on Earth if there is a lot of negativity about. They find it to be a barrier, preventing them from getting through and reaching us. Negativity makes such a heavy vibration. If you like, it can be compared to smog, and the Angels can't get to us through it because it's too dark and thick.

That's why we need to be mindful that our thoughts and our actions are positive and encourage Light to be spread more widely around us.

We are all made of Light.

Our soul, or Spirit, is Light Energy.

If we are very sick or very upset, our inner Light becomes dulled.

We must remember to try and keep our own personal Light as bright as possible so as the Angels can easily access us and "hang around" close by. If they can be nearer quicker, then they can help us more often and more easily.

The brighter we are ourselves, on a spiritual level, the more we will GLOW.

The Human Aura
Most humans cannot see this brightness with their own eyes, but our spiritual Light is there, nonetheless.

All around and completely within us. This can be proven by photographing us with a special type of equipment that can sense the Light and heat of our "Aura" – (or Personal Light).

Your Aura
You may be aware that our Aura has many colours within it but each colour is just a section of white light. Therefore we are basically surrounded with a sphere of white light at all times.

If you keep your energy and Personal Light bright as much as possible, then you will find that you will attract others who are equally bright.
Also, you may find that you attract some negative people at times. This is because their light is not very bright while they are feeling or behaving negatively, so they are drawn towards your Light.

They may hope to "suck" some of your Light Energy from you in order to increase their own fading brightness. It's like a moth being drawn to a flame.

Avoid Negativity within Your Environment

When, you might feel at one time or another, that someone who may be in your immediate environment – (talking to you or looking at you, or just being near you) is "sucking" or "stealing" your Light away, then remove yourself from their company.

If a person is talking to you and making you feel uncomfortable, then this is why. Normally they may have quite a lot of brightness themselves, but on this particular day they may be feeling a bit negative. They may be ill, depressed, or angry.

Suddenly you may notice that their topic of discussion is making you feel uncomfortable, or that they are looking at you in a negative way.

Their EYES may seem quite dark and empty. They say the eyes are the window to the soul, and I have never heard a truer word. If you want to know what's going on with a person, or who they are, or where they are coming from at that particular instance in time... then look at the EYES.

The darker the eyes, often the darker the soul.

I'm not talking about eye colour either.

A darkness that is evident, on a deeper level than the physical.

A person could have any colour eyes, but if you notice their eyes are JET BLACK and seem like a *VOID*, then don't look into their eyes. They'll "drain" you, like a vampire drains its victims.

They'll drain your valuable LIFE FORCE.
Because… they're in a negative headspace.
And it SHOWS.

Eliminating Negativity

So, you realize the person talking to you is very "dark" on this particular day. You may find yourself thinking: "I know that normally
they're a fairly cheerful and easy-going person, of course that's why
we are friends."

But at the moment their Light is dim.
You can sense a bit of negativity coming from them.

You may even feel yourself getting a headache.
This is because they are zapping your energy.
They are, perhaps even unconsciously - pouring a *"grey sludge of nega-
tivity over you"*.

You may genuinely feel concerned for them.

You may wish to ask them what's bothering them.
You might hope to be able to turn the discussion around into a positive
outcome, or you may chose to remove yourself.
Give it some serious thought
If you try to help them by talking about their problem, that's okay,
but make sure you *mentally "seal" or "protect" yourself from receiving/
absorbing their negativity.*

You may *"close yourself off"* this way using a mental force field.

By visualizing a sphere of **White Light** around your entire being, fully encompassing yourself, this will act as a bounce-off shield, to reflect out and away any negativity.

Remember, just like with clothing on a hot summer day...
White reflects, while black absorbs.

KEEP YOURSELF "WHITE & BRIGHT!"

If you *can* help your troubled friend, you may feel their negativity lightening up and you may end up even getting a smile or laughter out of them in the end. But if you feel they are not changing their "mood" or if you feel as though they are "draining" your Light Energy, just move away.

We all have good days and bad days, part of being human.
No-one is essentially EVIL; the dark is only providing contrast for us.
So we can recognize dark and light...
And can choose what we prefer.
Generally, if we want to be happy, then we choose...The Light.
When we are CONSCIOUS of our thought processes and AWARE of our mood.

Excuse yourself from negative people, when they are in that dark space.
Remove yourself, if you feel you have to... just move away from them for a while. If someone is "bringing you down," best to get out of there, anyway.

If it's' a family member or someone *very close*, still guard your aura, but of course you'll *want* to help if you can.

Family, loved ones, extremely close friends **will and can** spill over *some* negativity onto you, or drain your energy a little bit, but they aren't going to be ruthless in their "draining" of your Light, because they LOVE you.

Unlike a stranger, they won't take ALL your energy.
You have established a huge "bank account" of "GOOD ENERGY" with these people - because they love you and you love them.

You will take turns in helping each other at low points, being the listener, and the talker, the problem dumper, and the problem solver. But the little bit of Light that you drain from each other at times, and the negativity that you pour over each other at other times, is only minimal. Minimal, compared to the huge account you have built up over many years and much Love.

So there's not a deficit with these individuals, because there's a lot of Love and Light in reserve. Someone you love very much might tell you a big problem and they might cry and scream, and flip their lid about it... right on your shoulder and in your ear! Still, you'll handle it.

Because, the "unloading" or "negative downloading" plus "draining" process they zapped you with is worth, say, 50 units.

It hardly makes a dent in your "account" because they've deposited thousands and thousands of units into your account over your lifelong overall positive friendship or relationship.

But a stranger, they just want to withdraw. And a not so close person, they just want to withdraw.

No deposits previously. So… there's a deficit.

Emotional Vampires

It may sound weird, but I could also give this example:

Just like in the classic tales of horror that we all know, a "Vampire" will "feed" his friends and family from his *own* blood supply, and *drain theirs* too if he has to – (when reserves are low all around).

They need, if they have not "FED" for a while… to give their "own friends and family" a drink now and again; and they may allow these same close individuals to have a little "drink" from them as well, at times.

But they don't kill off their own kind.

Because that's "FAMILY".
A stranger on the street, however, is another matter!
Blood. Light. Life Force… anyway…

Hold fiercely onto your Light Energy and get out of the negative zone.

Avoid "Emotional Vampires".

AVOID NEGATIVITY.

Shine Brightly

Remember, Angels need Light to access us, so do all you can to keep yours always shining brightly, so that you can feel the Angels close by and know they are ready to help you.

Time Out! – "Off the Radar"

Sometimes it's hard to keep Bright. Day to day Life has an impact on us all, it takes your Light away and drains you. When you feel tired, exhausted or drained, sometimes it's advisable to *Slip Underneath the Radar*, so to speak. If you are feeling really worn out, and as though your energy or Light is being heavily taxed, try going Off the Radar.

This means, get some rest, regroup, centre yourself and stay in a peaceful environment. Take some TIME OUT, at home, have a big sleep, take your phone off the hook if you feel that you really don't want to be disturbed. Taking a break from the world is a healthy practice if you do it from time to time.

"Time Out" allows our *batteries to re-charge*, and a great big sleep can truly work miracles. Sleep tops up your inner Light, your soul, your energy, and it prepares you to face the world again.

Sleep/Rest

Sleep not only restores your physical health, but it tops up your Light supply.

Spending time with Mother Nature, walking in a park, smelling the wonderful smells of the plants and taking in the green foliage and the flowers many colours and energies can help to rejuvenate a tired spirit. Watching a sunset or sunrise is equally mellowing and restorative.

Sunrise

Watching a Sunrise is an incredible and beautiful experience. As the colours paint the horizon and spill upon the Earth, you can suddenly see a new day in its entire splendor.

For each Sunrise represents renewal, re-birth, and the beginning of a new day. It reminds us that each new beginning is filled with the potential for Beauty, Love and Light.

Sunset

Sunset is a peaceful time of acceptance, serenity and grace. It is the end of the day, symbolic of the end of every cycle. Sunset is breathtaking and grants us the gift of closure, of acknowledging that there is a time to rest ahead. Sunset is a time of truth, for asking for answers.

There is an old saying that if you look into the Sunset and ask the Universe for an answer, you can release your worries up to the Universe, in the knowledge that you will receive insight to your problem within the freshness of perspective that can be found in the new day and time ahead.

LIGHT UPON THE EARTH

Angels Love Light

Angels need Light.

Like we humans need air … to breathe.

Light… It transports them from the Cosmos onto the Earth Plane, to do their work.

The more Light we can visualize and get onto the Earth, the more the Angels can get here and be close enough to help in healing the "ills of the world". If we visualize the Globe, and where the Light is most needed here, we can further imagine columns of White Light from the Planet Earth, reaching up into outer Space...

We can help the Angels this way, to travel easier onto our Earth Plane and be manifest here upon the Earth.

Ground Zero

It is interesting to note that the tragedy of the September 11th Twin Towers in New York City has resulted in a "MONUMENT OF LIGHT" being created instead of some other type of solid memorial structure.

Devastation like that which occurred in that location and the huge number of lives affected by the destruction of the original towers may never be fully negated and healed. The sorrow that was thrust upon the lives of so many has expanded to affect us on a global level, with the overwhelming feeling of disappointment relating to the moral and ethical degeneration within certain aspects of society today.

However, I feel that no more fitting a monument could there possibly be, as the twin columns of Light that reach high into the skies over New York City are aiding in the healing process of the area affected and the spirits that were touched so heavily.

Both those that were lost and their grieving families can be aided in the comfort and healing process, over time of course, by the brilliant twin beams of Light that are released from the location.

It is interesting to note that the beams are bluish in hue…
Which is *the* most powerful HEALING COLOUR FREQUENCY
OF LIGHT.

Peace on Earth

It is hoped that the twin beams of Light will act as a transporter of
vast "armies" of Angels, who may use the Light to travel down onto
the area and aid those people affected in their healing process.

Also, that city in particular, and the general area that is Manhattan
Island, I would say may be the greatest candidate for any city on
the globe that may require healing and the assistance of our blessed
Angelic beings.

If the Angels can use those columns of Light to get onto the Earth and
start doing their work in that area, it would make a huge difference
to society and hopefully from that area could create a wave effect of
healing and compassion across the entire Globe of Earth.

A word about "Guardian Angels"…

We are all "allocated" a Guardian Angel when we come to be incarnate in human form on this Earth Plane. He is like our own personal
"Minder" or "Bodyguard".

He oversees us when we are asleep and keeps us safe from harm. Our
Guardian Angel is like the Imaginary Friend that children speak
about, that no-one can ever see.

Maybe kids *CAN* see their Angel? And we as adults tell them it's a lot
of rubbish. Children are supposed to be more finely tuned in to such
things, as are pets.

Your Guardian Angel is your best friend, but you can't see them.

But they are there.

Near you...
Always.

Trust in that.

Angels will always APPEAR...
When they are most needed.

Minutes, seconds...when it truly counts.

When all seems lost...

That is when angels respond suddenly to your emergency call...
On the L&L Inc. Network.

The call you make in your Mind - when you need them most.
The signal that your Heart emits.

When you really need a miracle.

And you're sure no-one can hear you.
Never give up!

Of course, the whiter and brighter you keep your Light Energy...
The closer they can come to you.

Affirmation for Brightness

"Keep your energy
White and bright
So the Angels may do their work
With delight
Keep it drawn in
Close and tight
Wrapped around
And increasing your Light."

AFFIRMATION

18

The Power of the Spoken Word

Affirmation is basically another form of "Prayer".

Or dialogue.

With Source.

But when you are "Affirming", you not only are addressing Source or God…
You are also ACTUALLY speaking to YOURSELF!

Your Higher Self.
Making an announcement to YOURSELF!

The Power of the Spoken Word.

That which holds the key - to mastering creation into physical form.
The infinite power and potential of Affirmation.

These two short words are extremely powerful words:
"I am…"

I am!
What this means is that you create a sentence or a group of sentences that are designed to affect your own mind.
You may speak as if you are speaking to yourself - in a mirror.
Basically your "Affirmation" is tailored specifically by you…
To program your own sub-conscious mind.
To open a file that says: "I WANT THIS!"
Yes – THIS is what I want!
See it Universe?
See what it looks like?
Got my special order?

HERE'S WHAT I WANT!
HERE - is my WISH manifest.

YES!
"Affirmative" means "YES".

This is where the word *"Affirmation"* comes from.

An Affirmation is therefore, a personalized script.

Either it can be repeated mentally or it can be spoken aloud.

It can be written down on paper; you may even like to make up signs with your Affirmation(s) written on them and stick these signs up around your house.
If you like, you can stick an Affirmation that may assist with weight loss, on your refrigerator.
You can stick an Affirmation to assist with better self-image on your bathroom mirror.

You can stick these "signs" up wherever you wish in your environment.
So that you see them often...
And repeat the Affirmation out loud several times daily.
Basically anywhere that you are bound to see them on a regular basis.

The more they are repeated, the greater their effect.

Guidelines:
For Affirmations to be successful there are two important guidelines to be aware of:

The First Rule of Affirmation:

1. Positive Language
Firstly... Affirmations must only be positive.

You are, in a way, almost hypnotizing yourself.

So ensure that your statement is a positive one, designed to encourage positive change.

The other reason for this is because both The Universe and the human mind are like a computer's "brain".

They respond to a direct task.

They cannot understand negative commands.

What this means is this:

It's like clicking to open a file on your computer.

The computer understands the instruction as "Open this file".

It would not understand an instruction that said "DON'T open this file."

Once you click… it "IS HAPPENING."

It is NOT – "NOT-HAPPENING!"

A computer only knows how to - DO, DO, DO!

So, when you say aloud "I am happy…"

You are in effect, calling up a "file" which represents, or is file-named/labeled:

"I am happy".

The brain, like a computer, only hears:

"Open the file that has to do with HAPPY."

"Search for things to do with *HAPPY, HAPPY, HAPPY!*"

So it searches for a file that contains information in it to do with…"HAPPY".

Magnetic Thoughts and Words

The mind is like a magnet, what you hold in your mind will be drawn towards you.

When you are calling up a "HAPPY" file, you are drawing this quality towards you, into your life.

It's like you want to open and run the "HAPPY" programme.

DOWN-LOADING "HAPPY" ... INTO YOUR SYSTEM.

Running the HAPPY software today!

But... If you say: "I am NOT SAD" –
(INSTEAD of: "I am HAPPY...")
Then the brain, like a computer, cannot understand it.
It doesn't comprehend negative instructions.

So the "brain" ignores the negative aspect of the command – (ie: "NOT") -

And searches instead, for a "mental file" containing the REST of the information.
It quickly finds the "SAD, SAD, SAD "programme and opens it, drawing the quality of sadness towards you.

Slotting that sadness chip in!
Installing and running the "sadness software" into your system.

DOWN-LOADING SAD...
INTO YOUR SYSTEM!

INTO YOUR BODY.
INTO YOUR EMOTION SLOT.
INTO YOUR LIFE.

Mind Your Language
So, be careful what you say.
Instead of saying: "I am NOT FAT", you must say… "I AM SLIM!"

Instead of saying: "I will NOT FORGET my appointment", you must say… "I REMEMBER my appointment!"

Otherwise, your brain only registers the command to "FORGET my appointment".

So remember… Absolutely NO negatives!
Keep it positive.

The Second Rule of Affirmation

2. Use Present Tense –
(The "NOW" Factor!)
The other thing that is vital to remember when it comes to the use of Affirmation…
Is related to the concept of "Time".

Time?
Past, present, future…
It is all the same thing.

There is no concept of "Time" when it comes to Affirmation.

From the moment you begin to Affirm towards achieving a result, you act as if you have already achieved it.

Act as if it is already happening.
Everything must be stated in the PRESENT tense.
The dandelion doesn't look at its watch as you blow it.
The flowers don't yell at the bee to hurry up and pollinate it!
For Mother Nature, there is no clock.
So Time is irrelevant.
It is only us as human beings, that obey the constraints of Time.
That buy into the chronological measurement trip.
That are overwhelmed with numbers... and what they are meant to represent!
In "Magic Land" - where wishes are made...
There are no digits, nor yesterday, or next week...
Just right now.

NOW... IS WHERE ALL MAGIC IS MADE.

If you want to be healthy, you say:
"I AM healthy".

If you want to be successful, you say:
"I AM successful".

Try to begin all your Affirmations with the words **"I am..."**

Personalize it.
Make it YOURS.
OWN IT!

Who Are You?

You are making a statement to the Universe about your *"authentic"* self.

About that which you aspire to be.

You are announcing information loudly to The Universe.
But also - and most importantly… to yourself.

It is similar to brainwashing yourself …
Into believing that the positive change is already happening.
So act as if it's already happening.
It will bring about an incredible result.

Align Yourself

You must try to *"align"* your vibration to that which you feel matches your *"wish"*.

By "aligning" it means trying to capture the feeling/emotion that accompanies your result being achieved.

If you want to improve your body, say: "I AM sexy, slim and desirable."
Try to act as though you are already those things.
How does it *"feel"* inside to be sexy, slim and desirable?

Harness that Feeling

Try to capture and harness that feeling of inner confidence.
By aligning your inner feelings with your aim you will magnetically draw it towards yourself. You will exude more inner "sexiness" and it will shine through.
It will be noticed by people…
Because your newfound radiance brightly attracts MORE *"good"* things towards you.

Remember, use **PRESENT** tense...

Bombard yourself with Affirmations of your choice, and start to act and feel as if it's already occurring. You'll be amazed how powerful an effect this combination will have - on both yourself and any others that you will come into contact with.

The Mirror Effect

Your positivity will magnetically radiate and attract more positivity; as if it is reflected straight back to you, like a mirror.

Your thoughts are a magnet...
Mind what you say and think!

VISUALIZATION

Prayer with Pictures

I see the 8-ball going into the corner pocket!
I am the winner.

Having discussed earlier how to engage a dialogue with Source &/or
The Universe...
I would now like to introduce another concept into the equation.

Visualization.
SEEING YOUR GOALS ACHIEVED, IN YOUR MIND'S EYE.

Visualization

When having normal prayer or dialogue with source, it is usually when you are fully alert, but relaxed, and only on a verbal level. (Using the example of your verbal or mental "meeting" with the L&L Inc. Board). Otherwise this is known as "prayer".

You can speak clearly and directly through your "open channel" to the Universe.
Or you mentally think of the words inside your head.

Announce your Truth!

A method you can incorporate into your communication with Source:
Visualization.

"Illustrations" to Accompany Prayer.
I guess, it's a prayer with pictures.
But before using pictures, you can use colour.

In order to do this you must first clear your mind of all the other distracting thoughts.

Clarity and Focus

Get clear, focus on *one* thing.
Clarity is vital.
When you are clear and focused – super sharp, your thought and Light Energy will be concentrated and shot out into the Universe like a laser beam.

Clarity equals highly concentrated Light
Focus equals intent, aimed at a result.

A Laser Beam, a Light Beam.

Think about it.

If you want to ask the Universe for help, you know that is one avenue you can take, but in a way you can assist it to help by adding some extra COLOUR into the scenario.

Colours can be used in SO many ways, according to the type of effect you are hoping to achieve.

Whatever it IS that you would like to achieve...
You must think first about the appropriate colour - to TRANSMIT your request out into the Universe with.

Performing a Healing Visualization
So, let's say you want to ask the Universe to help to aid in the healing process for a sick person. The person is a relative or friend who you know wants to get better - but is having some difficulty in healing quickly.

Sending Healing Energy
So you want to send healing energy along with your request to the Universe for healing. You want to send healing help.

Clarity: *You want the person to get better...*
Focus: *You want to concentrate on that objective and nothing else.*

But there are all these distractions around. Noises around, all these other thoughts in your mind. The "noises" around you distract you. So eliminate them.

"Turn Down The Other Senses:" Shhhhhh!

Eliminate everything else that will weaken your "channel" being clear and open. By minimizing the input received normally from the five *regular* senses, the "Sixth Sense" or "Open Channel" can be more easily *"tuned into"*.

1. Sound: Turn off the TV or radio or any noisy appliances. Close the window if the outside noise is too loud. Playing light, relaxing music can often help to set an appropriate mood.

2. Scent: If any strong smells are around, try to eliminate them. Burn some essential oils to make the room smell neutralized and relaxing. Frankincense is particularly good for relaxation and visualization.

3. Touch: Unlike prayer alone – (that can be done anywhere), make sure you are comfortable and totally relaxed to incorporate visualization. Lie down, relax, and lay on the couch or your bed, somewhere tranquil.

4. Taste: If you can taste some distracting taste like garlic or something that is hard to ignore, then drink some water to neutralize your taste-buds.

5. Sight: Close your eyes and let yourself drift away. You don't want to see with your regular "eyes" but you want to be able to see with "your mind's eye". They say this is within the realm of our imagination. The ability to "imagine" or "visualize" can sometimes be more easily accessed by focusing on the area between your eyes – or just above them, on the forehead.

This is meant to be the "third eye". It can't be seen with the other two eyes open. So close your eyes and relax.

If the environment feels relaxing now and there are no major distractions then you are ready to begin.

A special caution!

If you haven't already done so, take the telephone off the hook!

A ringing telephone in the middle of a relaxation technique such as this can be quite an unwelcome disturbance.

Relaxation / Meditation Technique
Close your eyes. Relax.
Address the Universe, your "Board Members:"

"Dear God, Angels, Helpers…etc."
Ask the Universe to empty your mind of all the other clutter.

Tell the Universe to please take all the stray thoughts, or "stuff" away and let you relax. Breathe deeply…

Listen to your breathing, concentrate on the sound of your breath.

As you relax you will notice your breathing becoming slower and deeper.

Feel your body and mind "slowing down" to take some "time-out".

If it's your Guardian Angel that you are going to "connect" with then you can fully relax yourself because you know they are going to help.

Entrust your "safety" whilst you're relaxing to your Guardian Angel.

Talk to your Guardian Angel
You may like to offer a traditional prayer.

Make connection with your Guardian Angel. The more communication you have with your Guardian Angel, the better you will feel you are getting to know them. If you Pray, Affirm, or Visualize more regularly, they will start to seem like an "old friend" to you. They always listen, and are always "there for you". It's quite a comforting notion.

So, "call" them, any time…
Day or night.

A Prayer to our Guardian Angel:

"Angel of God
My Guardian Dear
For whom God's Love
Commits me here
Ever tonight
Stay by my side
To love me and hold me
Protect me and guide me…
Amen."

*- So, now that you've handed yourself into
the care of your Guardian Angel...*

*Ask your Guardian Angel to help you focus on your task.
Recall your task and focus your thoughts.*

Speak to your Guardian angel, either verbally or mentally.

Ask them for what type of help you need.

*In this case, you would ask for your friend (the sick person) to receive
Healing from Source.
Ask your Guardian Angel to talk to the sick persons Guardian Angel.*

Speak about what you are focusing on.

*Say to your Guardian angel that he might communicate to the sick friends
Guardian Angel that you are not pushing the help upon them.*

*Be sure to say that you are simply ONLY OFFERING the help, should
they need or want extra help to get better.*

Help is on its way...
*So, if your friend really wants and needs extra healing, you would like to
help.
The Guardian Angels can act as go-between's. They can "work out" the
situation on your behalf. Almost like interpreters of the transmission.*

*Because that is what you're doing.
Sending out a transmission.*

Blue – The "Healing" Frequency

Visualize in your mind's eye the BLUEST Light you can imagine.

This is because blue is the healing colour and the task at hand is to send healing energy.

Blue light is coming from deep within your mind's eye; it comes from an endless Source.

It is streaming from your mind's eye out into the Cosmos.

Ask that the beam of blue light be directed to the sick person, with the assistance of the Angels.

"Angels please help me, using this Light I am sending out to you."

Angels travel and work via light, as we already know.

Visualize the blue Light encompassing the person requiring the healing. Imagine a picture in your mind of the person being well and happy again, energized and re-juvenated. Mentally affirm for the result you wish to obtain.

Say in your mind…
"YOU ARE WELL, YOU ARE HEALED, "

Affirmation is always in the PRESENT TENSE, as if it has already happened.

Feel within your entire being the power of the healing vibration.

Thank the Angels for their help.
Relax and return to being "grounded" again.
Wait until you feel ready; become aware of your own breathing again.
Open your eyes.

Welcome back to Earth
You may feel a bit "woozy" or light-headed for a few moments while you compose yourself back to reality.
That's why it's best to take the phone off the hook. If you were suddenly interrupted during such a visualization exercise – (say, by a ringing phone), you might feel a little out-of-it or disorientated for a moment.

This as I have just described, is the principle of Visualization.
Prayer with pictures and colours thrown in.

A more vivid way of getting your message TRANSMITTED out there.

Tailor your "own" Visualizations
You can incorporate *any colour of light* that you need into a visualization of your own, as long as the colour corresponds with the type of energy you are hoping to transmit out.

Based on the earlier *"Colour Symbol Chart"* in this book you can choose the colour vibration that best "lends" itself to the result you wish to achieve.

Based upon our "Healing Visualization", there is a formula for this type of task, and I will illustrate it with the use of symbolism previously established in this book.

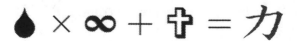

The "Visualization Formula" can be adapted to any type of Visualization or prayer; but in this case, the symbol of the "cross" is the "healing" symbol, (associated with the energy of Blue Light).

Dialogue or Monologue?

I've previously referred to Prayer and Visualization as a "Dialogue with The Universe", but you may think that is strange. Because in ordinary terms, a DIALOGUE is a conversation or communication between Two Parties, where *BOTH* contribute.

Otherwise, you might think that prayer is somewhat more of a MONOLOGUE. I beg to differ!

Prayer is most definitely a DIALOGUE. Even though you may not immediately HEAR or RECEIVE an instant answer or reply, if you are patient and hold your Faith, in due course you *will* receive a reply.

For every TRANSMISSION, there is a RECEIPT.

So a *DIALOGUE* is about TRANSMITTING and RECEIVING.

Shortly you will learn how to be aware of "signals" that may indicate that your Transmission has been received by the Universe. It's all about being "aware" and "open", to receiving, and recognizing opportunities.

Watch the Radar

Stay open, keep watching the Radar, and wait...

Hold your Faith, be patient, just relax and be cool. What will be, will be.

Sharpen your "Antennae" and prepare to become a RECEIVER.

COMMUNICATION

20

Technology Vs. "The Heart"

So...

We know that our senses, particularly our "Sixth Sense" or OPEN
CHANNEL...
Sends us or sensually offers us –
Messages.

About ourselves, our lives, our underlying "feelings" and our "emotions".

And we also know that these emotional currents can, over a period of time and build-up, result in powerful ENERGY being harnessed and released for an effect.

We know …
That we can focus and direct this energy out into the Universe to achieve a result.

So, we now know how to send out our TRANSMISSIONS.

Our messages, our contributions, our energies, our Light.

But can we receive transmissions back?
How can we become RECEIVERS?

Not just of our *own* messages – our INTERNAL INFORMATION – (ie: underlying emotional currents as interpreted through our own senses)…

But, RECEIVERS of EXTERNAL messages.

We would ideally like to be able to know how to *RECEIVE TRANSMISSIONS BACK - from external sources.*

We want Replies.

We'd love to know that our messages are getting out there.
We'd like answers…
But how?

Once Upon a Time…

Once we had… Carrier Pigeons.

How advanced!

So - what if your pigeon got mixed up… and took your letter to the wrong window?

"I am madly in love with you. Will you marry me?"

Instead of going to your beloved Prince Charming, the pigeon got a bit confused.

So your note gets delivered to the town hunch-back's house by mistake…

Talk about hanging out to see if your pigeon came back with a reply note tied to its leg?!

Worse still, the town hunch-back says in his reply note:
"Yes, of course I'll marry you!"

You say to yourself, "Hang on!

This doesn't look like my Prince's hand-writing AT ALL!

(Ohhh NO! Help)…*What's going on?"*

But then again, maybe the pigeon knew exactly what he was doing after all?

Maybe the town hunch back is actually the man of your dreams?

Your Destiny. Who knows?

Mother Nature is funny like that.

Destiny

"Destiny" is a strange concept. It is meant to represent our hearts deepest and most fulfilling desires. It's about our dreams. Finding our "place to belong" in the world.

Some people think they have a fair idea what their destiny is, but they grow impatient. They can't wait for it to arrive in its own time-frame, so they try to do things that they think are going to speed it up or bring their *"imagined" Destiny* closer, quicker.

But apparently, Destiny *cannot* be rushed. Nor pressured, nor anticipated.

Your Destiny… *comes to YOU!*

If you try to move closer to it, it just seems to get further away.

You just have to sit tight, in fact, put it right out of your mind. Concentrate on other things. Throw yourself into activities. "Work" is great… It's a perfect "distraction" for so many billions of people around the Globe.

A *productive* distraction. Actually, to work, is a fantastic way to… "lose yourself" in something.

Even better if your work gives you a great deal of spiritual satisfaction.
A LABOUR OF LOVE! Ideal.

To feel you are making a positive contribution to society, as well as benefiting yourself. If you can GIVE on so many levels, and DRAW on so many varied and beautiful aspects of Life, then it's a healthy exchange of energy. Everyone's benefiting… WIN/WIN!
It *has* to be.

And… of course, it's earning money, which helps to bring you greater financial freedom, and more opportunity. The more people you come into contact with each day, the more opportunity you encounter, the more you can quickly recognize, the more you can explore, the more chance you have of meeting your Destiny...

It will come to you when you are least expecting it.
Just keep it REAL. Keep it POSITIVE. Keep it all about Love and Light.

Follow Your Heart.

Communication in the New Millennium

Based on our earlier example, we *had* to come up with something more reliable than carrier pigeons! So later, the two tin-cans arrived, with a piece of string attached at each end to a can...

"Hello? Hello? Can you HEAR me?"

And so, it further developed, and the telephone was born.
Thank God for *that* invention!

Let's explore four examples of today's methods, based upon proven, currently used technology.

How far *have* we come from trained pigeons and the "string-can-a-phone"?

Postal: You send a letter or a parcel to someone. It's very important, so you send it by Express Post and you make it "Person-to Person". You may have to pay an extra fee for this facility but it's important that you ensure it goes directly to that person. It could be a confidential letter, let's say. So, the process of delivery in this case ensures that the right person gets it, because the mail man has to get them to provide a signature and identification upon receipt. If you really want to be sure the person has received it, you can get the postal service to rip off the signed piece of card and mail it back to the senders address. This is called "confirmation of receipt". You get the card back, signed, so you are satisfied that the item was received. Done.

Telephone: You dial the phone and the person answers. Even if they don't answer, you can often leave a message on their voice-mail or answering machine. Usually if the person answers, you know pretty quickly if it is the person you wanted to speak to. If it isn't, then it may be a wrong number, so you try again. In any case, if they aren't available at that time you can leave a message. When they call you back, you then know that they came home or back to their office, heard the message, and your message was received. You know this because they call you back at their earliest convenience... (assuming that they are courteous and professional). So, your message was received. Over and done with.

Texting: You want to send a message to your friend by Text Message or via SMS – ("Short Message Service"). These are sent using mobile telephones, usually. You type the message out and you follow the prompts and enter the person's mobile number. The screen on your phone will ask you what you want to do next. If you are ready to send the message you press the button for "SEND". As the message is disappearing into cyberspace, your screen will alert you to the fact that your message has been sent. It will say in capital letters "Message Sent". You know it has been received because it can't just disappear into space. It is sent directly to the holder of that telephone number. Next time they look at their mobile phone they will notice a warning that says "Message Received" and will prompt them to open and read their new message. It often features a facility to enable them to reply or store that message. They can also choose to delete the message, but in any case, it is received. If they send a reply you can be even more satisfied that they clearly understood your message transmission. Roger, ten-four...over....

E-MAIL: Electronic Mail. THE WORLD CONNECTED IN A SIMPLE CLICK!

You are working away on your computer and you need to send an important document to a person on the other side of the world. Even if you mailed it, it would take too long; it has to be there *yesterday*, or in other words... URGENTLY.

So you write them an E-mail message and attach the document as a file, it can be a video, music, text, whatever. You're sending it to them via E-mail, that is, through the Internet.

The Internet is a gigantic worldwide network where every computer on-line is...
Linked up and accessible.
It's like the L&L Inc. Network — but it's a "Material Form" Network. All linked up MOSTLY by optical fibres running underneath the ground.

But it also utilizes satellites in space to bounce information across oceans.

So in some ways, it is partially NON-FORM.

Part of this process relies on signals being beamed by light!

You need passwords to get in or out of your E-mail "INBOX" -

So it is equipped with encryption technology.

Certain files can also be encrypted for added security.

Virtually translated into secret code and then unscrambled at the recipients end by the Receiver.

So even if it's a "Super Confidential" file or document...

You can take additional steps to protect the security of the information.

Once the user clicks on the word "Send" - an E-mail is sent out into the world...

Of computer networks – (much like a giant WEB of exchanged information).

You know it is received because it comes up as listed in your "Sent Items" folder.

If there is any error in sending it, an independent E-mail comes through to you...

Advising you of the inability to deliver it to the correct address.

Otherwise, you can be assured that the message has been sent and received.

If a reply should be forthcoming, you can even gain feedback from there on.

Roger...ten-four...*over and out!*

If the signals can suddenly take a non-material form, and be transmitted into space …
Via light-beams, and be bounced back by the giant mirror of a satellite in space —

Then obviously…

INFORMATION DOES NOT HAVE TO BE IN A SOLID FORM TO BE SENT OR RECEIVED.

Just like in our Mind's eye, we can create the L&L Inc. Network and strengthen it…

We can use it to send our thoughts, hopes and dreams…
We can use crystals to store and magnify energy and thought.
We can mentally project brilliant laser-like beams… so that Angels can travel along the light.
Carrying our signals…
To God/Source.

And… to one another.

We can form the Light Network – With our MIND'S EYE!

TODAY…

- ✦ We have E-mail…
- ✦ Bluetooth - (the step into a different colour frequency than Infra-red to transmit data)…
- ✦ GPS, we can be a tiny speck on the Earth detected by satellites in space.

Information is CONTINUOUSLY beaming here and there all around us invisibly…

Through an invisible and Universal Web of Light.

So –

Are we ACTUALLY ALL linked by an INVISIBLE NETWORK OF LIGHT?

Maybe we ARE!

Perhaps we have simply forgotten how to connect?

How strong is YOUR signal?

Are YOU connected to the L&L Inc. Invisible Wireless Network?

Is your Heart the key - to logging on and utilizing the network?

And what drives it? *Electricity?*

But you don't literally PLUG yourself into anything to power yourself up… do you?

So maybe God, Source, or the great Cosmic Spirit…

Is - IN FACT… the Power - that drives this Invisible Network?

The Power that drives the Software of Humanity.

Maybe, quite possibly. We are ALL "ONE".

Humanity.

IS IT COSMIC SPIRIT THAT DRIVES OUR HUMAN MINDS & HEARTS…

AS WE THINK AND FEEL, AND EXPERIENCE… DURING THIS LIFETIME?

It is possible. Imagine it.

One Love!

Back to the Heart

Based upon our knowledge of currently used technology and methods of communication, we know that when we send out a message transmission via Post, Telephone, Text/SMS/MMS, or even E-mail, we can confirm that our transmission is received. So we send out an information transmission and we can subsequently take receipt of "reply" information.

So, when you send out a transmission into the Cosmos, based on only the methods of Prayer, Visualization, Affirmation and the like – (ie: non-technology based methods of "communication"), how can you know it's GETTEING THERE?

How do you know it's been heard, felt, intercepted and comprehended?

With The Human Mind and Heart

Although it's a bit different to the modern methods of our currently used technological examples, when we send out a transmission, it IS being received.

We *won't* get a little pink "delivery confirmation" card back in the mail, NOR will we get a message saying "Message Sent" suddenly glowing across our foreheads in neon letters.

So, how can we know?

We know, ON THE DEEPEST LEVEL… by listening to our own Self.

By holding our Faith.
By listening to our Heart.

I *don't* mean we have to stick a stethoscope on and literally listen to our chest.

I *mean* that we must "tune in" to the feelings we hold deepest within ourselves.

We must TRUST in ourselves to know the answer on some "immeasurable" level.

We just KNOW it, we feel it deep inside, in our gut, in the deepest part of our being.

Our Heart.

We just *believe*. Without proof... (We don't *need* proof).
We trust in the infinite potential of The Universe. We trust in *ourselves.*
Trust in those who trust in us.
Trust in the Universe in its' Infinite Wisdom.

We must give it up to The Universe, to God. Hand it over.

Let it go!
Surrender it up the Universe.
Release it.
Be liberated from the UNECCESSARY worry, wonder, and expectation.

"Relinquish the need to demand explanations...
And believe in the strength and power of our own Heart."

Our Heart...
Our Spirit. Source. Our Mind, our TRUEST self!

Signs

You could go "bonkers" if you were looking too hard for answers, but it doesn't hurt to be aware of what's going on around you as you wander your path.

Just have your Antennae open.

KEEP AN OPEN MIND.

Sometimes we are given or shown little signs that indicate to us that we are on the right path, or that our message has been heard and the answers or solutions are indeed on their way. You can receive messages in lots of different ways, as long as you are open to recognizing and meditating upon their message.

Here are some examples:

1) *Music, TV, Media and the Arts –*
2) *Birds, Animals, Nature, Plants,*
3) *People you know; and …*
4) *People you might meet along the way.*

Nature and Animals

You're looking for answers, but there's no help coming yet. So you go for a walk in the park.

Nature relaxes you, and your mind wanders. You may see things from a different perspective; you may be inspired by the colours of the flowers and the behaviour of the birds that you see while on your walk. A bird might fly up and perch itself before you. You wonder if it has a message for you. Birds often bring "news". (They are the spiritual descendants of the "Carrier Pigeon", after all). And let's not forget about the "Stork!"

Where Life Imitates Art

You are still looking for a solution.

You might go to an exhibition of art, and the art may move you.

You may find a painting speaking to you, it is hypnotically affecting you. You connect with the spirit of the subject matter and find yourself lost in another dimension.

The painting might offer you through its imagery, a message for your Soul.

Media Messages

You might turn on the TV, and there's a programme you really NEEDED to see. Within it may lay a special clue to solving your problem.

Music & Song

You might hear a song, and the words sung will speak to you of another's "Life Experience". You may find that you strangely "connect" with the sentiment. It may "hit a nerve", "press a button", trigger a profound reaction inside you.

It may make you feel emotional, because it's giving you a message. It asks you to search deep inside yourself, and see what you can come up with. How can you apply the lesson or teaching of the song to your own Life?

Thinking Too Hard

Insomnia. No-body likes this one. We've ALL suffered from this at times.

And the main reason we are unable to sleep...

Is usually a subconscious WORRY that is running rampant around and around, without an obvious solution.

That's why if people can't make an important decision:
People often will say...
"I need to sleep on it!"
Hoping that the new and fresh perspective of morning might shed new light onto a baffling situation.

Insomnia:
It's a HUGE signpost that something is worrying you, in fact it's eating away at you.

Ask the Universe to "turn off your brain" for a while, to take your problem off your hands...

Hand it over to a higher power and breathe deeply.
In the peaceful knowing that a solution WILL be shown to you.

Trust in the Universal Processes.

STEP OUT OF YOUR PROBLEM:
It is NOT YOU.
It is only a segment of your life.
Put it aside.

Did you ever wander along, your head heavy with a problem, virtually unaware of the rest of the world?

Did you ever find that you were so immersed in your "problematic" thoughts that you were almost oblivious to those around you?

That you were completely zoned out?

That no-one could reach you if they wanted to? That you are so pre-occupied with your own thoughts that you can't even concentrate on simple tasks, or anything else?

Snap out of it!

It's difficult to help someone, if you can't even get their attention!

SHIFT YOUR FOCUS OFF THE PROBLEM...
AND BACK ONTO THE REST OF YOUR HORIZONS.

"Undercover Angels"
Angels can blend in with us sometimes, in human form.
They appear to give us little snippets of information and advice.
But often, they blend in so well, they may appear so insignificant, that we might walk straight past them without ever looking closely enough.

Did you ever have the experience of meeting someone in the street, whom you felt compelled to listen to?

You might have been thinking "I don't even KNOW you"...
Yet you just felt as though you should stop and talk to them, to listen to what they were saying. Maybe they had a funny hat on or something? The "funny hat" got your attention, anyway. Maybe it had a big purple flower stuck on it, and you *love* the colour purple?

It could be a little old lady who seems to be rambling on ridiculously, nothing really making sense, just chitter-chatter about something insignificant.

Then, all of a sudden, she says something completely "wacky", like this:

"You know...I looked under the bed once. And you won't believe what I found! A tiny little scrunched up bit of paper that I've been looking for. It has my grand-daughter's phone number on it. Can you believe it? I've been hunting around for that bit of paper for years now!"

You might think to yourself...
"Good for you, so you found the bit of paper. Whoopee-do!"

But all of a sudden you have a "flash" of break-through!
"Right. Under the bed! Maybe that's where I have to look for my lost bracelet? The one that belonged to my Grand-mother and I haven't been able to find for years now."
So you turn around to thank the old lady, and what? She's GONE. No-where to be seen. And you think to yourself... *"Who WAS that little old lady?"* Weird huh?
That's an "Undercover Angel" for you.

There one second, then disappeared... in the blink of an eye.

So keep your eyes wide open.

And never underestimate the importance of being "open".

Guarded, certainly.
But "open".

Remember:
The Universe sends us valuable clues and little snippets of information, through the most unlikely and unexpected means.

But... In order to receive information and answers from the Universe, you MUST detach from the issue!

GIVE IT UP TO THE UNIVERSE.
HAND IT OVER FOR A WHILE.

IMPORTANT!

IT CAN'T TRANSMIT YOU ANY ANSWERS WHILE YOU'RE SO BUSY "JAMMING UP THE LINE!"

If you think about an issue non-stop, you are sending out transmissions all the time in thought waves, and therefore the Celestial Transmission cannot get through to you with an answer.

In order to receive guidance or insight from the Universe, you HAVE to put your problem out of your mind, giving it back, or up... to the Cosmos.

Release it. Simply *know* in your mind and heart, that it will all work out fine.

It'll all be cool.
Chill out.
Let it go for a while.
Trust in a Higher Power.

TRUST!
Because, believe me...

Mother Nature's got it covered.
So, CHILLAX!
And don't forget to smile.
It helps bring about a good result FASTER.

Happy attracts happy.

And smiles… reflect smiles… reflect smiles…

SMILES REFLECT SMILES REFLECT SMILES… to the power of infinity.

Plus one! (LOL) Plus one times infinity, etc.

In fact: INFINITY TIMESED BY THE POWER OF INFINITY…

IF IT EXISTS?! Infinity squared???

Silly numbers… that PROBABLY don't really exist.

But lighten up… and now that you get the idea.

Keep smiling!

KEEP LOGGED ON TO L&L INC.

AND REMEMBER WE ARE ALL ONE.

My pain is your pain.
My joy is your joy.
My love is your love.
My light is your light.

Ride the waves bravely…

And know that you are NEVER alone in this Life experience.

- *It has been said*
- *Felt*
- *Seen*
- *Written about*
- *Sang about*

+ *Fashioned into clay*
+ *Dreamed of*
+ *Created...*

- *By the many who came before.*
- *And the many who will come after.*

And YOU, and I.

Our Experiences recorded for all time...
Stored in the giant server...

For us to retrieve our memories from -

And run our programmes within this Lifetime.

Log on, smile, stay happy and give gratitude...
For the privelege and honour -
Of taking Human Form.

BLUEPRINTS

21

Creating Your "Script"

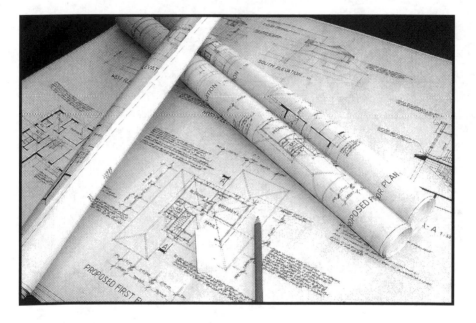

A Final Word...

In offering this book I hope that the information I have presented will be helpful to you. I hope it can be taken on-board to assist you in creating better harmony within your world.

With the use of Prayer, Affirmation and Visualization, you can bring about greater results and feel a new sense of security in the knowledge that The Universe, the Cosmos, HEARS your request.

Creating a Blueprint

I have demonstrated how Visualization can give a clearer *"Blueprint"* to the "Cosmic Spirit". That which we otherwise know as the Universe, Source, or God, a SPIRIT OR FORCE that is COSMIC, originating from the Stars…

By including colour, and even "pictures", images held in your mind's eye, you can present your "wish" on *SO* many levels. Not just in writing or words, or thoughts… but also in other methods.
Spoken word, focused thought, the use of imagery, pictures, colours of Light…

Clearly presenting your Blueprint.

That way, your personal "WISH" can become… the Manifestation of Cosmic Spirit!

Through purest of Light, and be ever-mindful of the vibration and power of Love.

For Love is All.
The Highest Power.

I referred to Blueprints earlier in these pages and likened them to IMAGINING.
Like the Architect who wants to design the new Library Building.

He wants to make it exceptional.

He wants it to last, to stand proud and tall.

He DOESN'T want cracks, wonky walls, and a dreary looking eyesore!
SO BUILD YOUR BLUEPRINTS IN YOUR MIND'S EYE...
With the Highest of Intentions.
Make your visions beautiful.

FEEL THEM AS YOU SEE THEM...
DESIGN FROM THE HEART!

Blueprints or "Scripts"
Here I have included some Affirmations/Visualizations or "scripts"
that you may wish to explore...
These show the formulae behind the process of creation:
So you can see how the energy moves, and what type of energy it is.
Thus: the energy of the "results" should always match those of its
"ingredients".

THIS IS... I suppose one might say... THE FORMULA BEHIND
MAGIC.

Yes that's right... ACTUAL MAGICAL SUMS!
(Magic wands are optional!)

Shhhhhhhhh... Or else everyone will be doing it shortly!

Remember always to smile when performing magic.

In fact:
"LOSLTEAWTNTWWWYALASWABDTKSTTCJIWTF"...
(Laugh Out So Loudly That Everyone Around Within The Nearest

Town Will Wonder What You Are Laughing At So Wildly And Be Desperate To Know So That They Can Join In With The Fun)!

Come on... get with it!
Surely you must have heard THAT one before?
Maybe someone texted it to you?
It's SO much more interesting than "LOL!"

Laughter, my friend, is ALWAYS the most magical healer of all.

Enjoy creating your own wish scripts and magical blueprints.

Remember: It all begins in the Heart and Mind.

3 EXAMPLES FOLLOW:

Enjoy them.

Healing

HEALING:

*"Candlelight
Burning bright
Aid me in this
Healing rite
Lapis lazuli
Sky and sea
All these are
The same to me
Purifying
Shades of blue
Pacifying
Make as new
Sapphire light
Aquamarine
Spares this Soul
Of all unclean."*

L<small>OVE</small>

$$\spadesuit \times \infty + \heartsuit = \heartsuit \text{力}$$

LOVE:

"Perfectly pink
Like the flush of my cheek
As it floods with the hue
Of happiness true
All encompassing
Spirit of Love
The elixir of Life…
All below and above
May my cup overflow
May I draw from the well
Of Eternity's Love
In the places I dwell
Through the journeys I make
'Midst the Angels I meet…
From the dawning of sunrise
'Til day is complete…
When I gaze to the Heavens
To welcome starlight
May I see only Love
As the moon heralds night
And as I behold
Love's rose in full bloom
May I entertain bliss
Through its' magic perfume."

PROSPERITY

$$\text{\Large $\blacklozenge$} \times \infty + \$ = \$ 力$$

PROSPERITY:

"I plant these three gold coins
Deep into the Earth
Of the sacred Money Tree
Grant me the gift
Of the Freedom of Wealth
And Blessed Prosperity
As the candle anointed
With Essence of Lemon
Burns with powerful flame
And the Jade Plant thrives
Bringing lustrous growth
So shall grow my finances the same
Each time that I shall talk with
And lovingly water
And tend to my beautiful tree
So shall my security
Expand and develop
By the grace of the Powers that be."

DO YOU HAVE A MONEY TREE?

"The Money Tree" - One might ask:
Is there such a thing as a Money Tree?

You will find it in the windows and entrances to many shops and businesses. It's good "Feng Shui".

The Chinese believe… If you should like to introduce greater prosperity and success into your environment, keep a Jade Plant near the entrance to your home/shop.

"The Jade Plant - (or Giant Jade) has always been associated with money!"

Ask the Universe to manifest your vision, or give you something even *better*, for the greatest good of all concerned.

Explain to God, The Universe, the Angels and Helpers **why** you need the money. Describe your *good intentions*, which will ensure it is used in a positive way based entirely on Love and Light.

Hold your vision clearly and align your vibration to that of wealth, prosperity and growth, as you light your candle. Allow your candle to burn down as you continue to re-affirm your goal. Re-light it often to continue releasing its energy…

EVERYONE SHOULD PLANT A MONEY TREE…
FOR AS ONE WATCHES IT GROW,
NATURE'S ABUNDANCE & GROWTH BECOMES CLEARLY
EVIDENT…
BEFORE ONE'S VERY OWN EYES!

Creating your own "Scripts"

I've included the Formulae, so that you can see what the "ingredients" are. You will notice that the "Colour Themes" will correspond with the type of "Energy" required.

Afterwards, get creative and positive. Have fun in formulating your *OWN Blueprints*, tailored to meet your personal visions of the Future.

Based always upon the rock-solid foundation of Love and Light.

This may assist in your "writing your *OWN* formula", to promote greater Happiness and Harmony.

In creating your "Blueprint for Happiness"...

Remember:
Everyone's vision of Happiness is Unique!
Be true to yourself.

Whatever your own personal vision may be...
Good luck with your Blueprint.

Manifest...
Through the power of Love and Light.
Make a wish!
May you see it complete.

Love can move mountains.
Love can always create Light where previously there was darkness.
You are a creator. An Architect of Light...

A magnet and a mirror for all that you see in your reality.

You are a perfect child of the Cosmos.
Look to that inner child and remember why you came here...
What would you like to create?
Make it exceptional.

The Directors at L&L Inc would be SO proud of your creations.

Do it - to prove it to yourself that you are made of the right stuff.

Are you ready - to step up... for your "promotion" in Life?

Love & Light Inc. Connectivity

Remember... at any given time you are connected to Love and Light Incorporated. You need only to relax and focus your mind to "log on" to the spiritually powered "wireless light network."

Visualize the light beams in your mind's eye and send your emotional and mental data out into the web of Cosmic Ether...

+ You may like to practice visualization – Prayer with Pictures.

+ You may speak proudly and passionately in the positive, present tense to Affirm to the Universe what you wish to draw into your reality.

+ You may send love and healing with your formula in mind as a blueprint, through beams of mentally created light.

- You may like to call a Board meeting and summon with your mind's eye the Angelic Light Workers that are busily working for L&L Inc.

- You may hold a meeting in your mind with them and express your needs and desires with an audience that you trust is hearing you. So you know in your heart L&L Inc. has heard and acknowledged your prayer or request.

- Think of your loved ones often and send light along the light beams in your mind's eye.

- The network of Light is being continuously created and strengthened by all who use and visualize it. Forever the light will remain so that the Web of Light is constructed firmly and is maintained by the like-minded… for the free and on-going use of all of Our Family at "L&L Inc."

Remember that you worked for Love and Light Incorporated long before your present human incarnation, and try to recall the task that was assigned to you when you were to be born into human flesh form.

Your human mind is simply the driver for the software that was installed in our systems long before this human experience.

We all have the capacity to link on to the network, we just have to remember how to activate the software and utilize the network of Light that spans across the entire Cosmos.

A web of light created eons ago, that has faded and collapsed due to lack of use and neglect… that can be recreated and re-enforced by the power of our human mind.

NO wires, no contracts…
Just YOU, with the Universe at your fingertips!
Close your eyes, breathe deeply, and re-connect yourself…

With the INVISIBLE Light Network.

Good luck and many blessings!

May you weave your own brand of magic - and be true to yourself.

Smile, breathe… and trust.

End Transmission!